450 Decorative Borders You Can Paint

NORTH LIGHT BOOKS
CINCINNATI, OHIO
www.artistsnetwork.com

450 Decorative Borders You Can Paint.
Copyright © 2005 by Jodie Bushman. Manufactured in China. All rights
reserved. The patterns and drawings in this book are for the personal use
of the decorative painter. By permission of the author and publisher, they
may be either hand-traced or photocopied to make single copies, but
under no circumstances may they be resold or republished. It is permissi-
ble for the purchaser to paint the designs contained herein and sell them
at fairs, bazaars and craft shows. No other part of this book may be repro-
duced in any form or by any electronic or mechanical means, including
information storage and retrieval systems, without permission in writing
from the publisher, except by a reviewer, who may quote brief passages in
a review. The content of this book has been thoroughly reviewed for
accuracy. However, the author and publisher disclaim any liability for any
damages, losses or injuries that may result from the use or misuse of any
product or information presented herein. It is the purchaser's responsibili-
ty to read and follow all instructions and warnings on all product labels.

Published by North Light Books, an imprint of F+W Publications, Inc.,
4700 East Galbraith Road, Cincinnati, Ohio 45236. (800) 289-0963.
First edition.

Other fine North Light Books are available from your local bookstore,
art supply store or direct from the publisher.

09 08 07 06   5 4 3 2
Distributed in Canada by Fraser Direct
100 Armstrong Avenue
Georgetown, ON, Canada L7G 5S4
Tel: (905) 877-4411

Distributed in the U.K. and Europe by David & Charles
Brunel House, Newton Abbot, Devon, TQ12 4PU, England
Tel: (+44) 1626 323200, Fax: (+44) 1626 323319
Email: mail@davidandcharles.co.uk

Distributed in Australia by Capricorn Link
P.O. Box 704, S. Windsor NSW, 2756 Australia
Tel: (02) 4577-3555

Library of Congress Cataloging-in-Publication Data
Bushman, Jodie
    450 decorative borders you can paint / Jodie Bushman.
        p. cm.
    Includes index.
    ISBN 1-58180-690-6 (hc : alk. paper)--ISBN 1-58180-691-4 (pbk)
    1. Painting--Technique. 2. Decoration and ornament. 3. Borders,
    Ornamental (Decorative arts) I. Title: Four hundred fifty decorative
    borders you can paint. II. Title.

TT385.B87297 2005
745.7'23--dc2
                                        2004028948

Editor: Holly Davis
Cover designer: Clare Finney
Interior designer: Amy F. Wilkin
Production Coordinator: Kristen Heller
Interior Layout Artist: Amy F. Wilkin
Photographers: Tim Grondin and Christine Polomsky
Photo Stylist: Nora Martini

fw
F+W PUBLICATIONS, INC.

About the Author

Jodie Bushman's painting career began in 1970
with an art course at a local college. She has been
painting ever since. Jodie has been an Associate
Designer for Delta Paint, and her artwork is
frequently published in popular painting magazines.
450 Decorative Borders You Can Paint is Jodie's
second North Light book, following *The Big Book of
Decorative Borders*. The borders and embellishments
in both books are the culmination of her many
years of design creativity. When she is not teaching
at seminars and conventions across the country,
Jodie can be found at her own Rainshadow Studio
at the base of beautiful Mt. Hood in Oregon,
where she lives with her husband, John.

Metric Conversion Chart

to convert	to	multiply by
Inches	Centimeters	2.54
Centimeters	Inches	0.4
Feet	Centimeters	30.5
Centimeters	Feet	0.03
Yards	Meters	0.9
Meters	Yards	1.1
Sq. Inches	Sq. Centimeters	6.45
Sq. Centimeters	Sq. Inches	0.16
Sq. Feet	Sq. Meters	0.09
Sq. Meters	Sq. Feet	10.8
Sq. Yards	Sq. Meters	0.8
Sq. Meters	Sq. Yards	1.2
Pounds	Kilograms	0.45
Kilograms	Pounds	2.2
Ounces	Grams	28.3
Grams	Ounces	0.035

Acknowledgments

I would like to thank Holly Davis and Kathy Kipp for making a tedious job fun. A special thanks to "Precious Tim," the step-by-step project photographer, for tolerating my silliness for one solid week. Thank you to my friends, students and strangers for all your kind words about my first book. I appreciate those words very much.

Dedication

I dedicate this book to my painting friends and students, and to those pioneers, no longer with us, who gave so much to our art form. Those pioneers are missed, but their legacy will live on, and memories of them are special to me.

Table *of* Contents

Introduction

450 Decorative Borders You Can Paint is my second book devoted to borders. As with my first book, *The Big Book of Decorative Borders*, my intent is to provide a large reference of borders and embellishments that artists can use in their work. As with the first book, this one includes basic techniques, several step-by-step projects, a collection of three-step borders and a gallery of hundreds of borders you can copy or use as inspiration. But one book does not replace the other.

For one thing, the two books offer wholly different sets of borders and border projects. With the two books, you can have a library of about a thousand borders and embellishments!

This second book also covers some different territory. I've introduced a few techniques, such as designing a project (pages 14-15) and positioning borders on scrapbook pages (page 54). I've also introduced different surfaces in this book, such as fabric and several paper types. (I had great fun with the border paper!) As you can see from the Table of Contents, each project addresses a specific bordering technique or painting surface.

By demonstrating different techniques and working with different surfaces, I've shown how adaptable borders are. Try using borders in ways not mentioned in either of my books—on name tags or labels, on ornaments or wrapping paper, on chairs, tables or cabinets. I'm sure you can come up with ideas of your own. Use your imagination and favorite colors, and surprise yourself with how creative you can be.

Chapter 1 Materials

Paint and Mediums

Projects in this book are painted with Delta acrylics. Delta produced the first acrylic paint on the market and the first I ever used. The advantages of these paints are that they are fast drying and not as toxic as oils.

Delta has acrylic paints appropriate for various surfaces. Most of the projects in this book are painted with Delta Ceramcoat Acrylics. Other types of Delta acrylics are introduced in the appropriate project materials list.

Paint mediums give paint special qualities. With Delta Ceramcoat Textile Medium, you can convert acrylic paint into fabric paint. I use Delta Ceramcoat Acrylic Thinner for linework because it doesn't break down the paint binder as water does. Some painters dip their brushes into retarder before starting to paint for the day. This helps in brush cleaning by preventing paint buildup at the ferrule.

Brushes

I recommend buying the best brushes you can afford. With proper care and cleaning, they'll serve you a long time. I have brushes I've used for ten years! On the other hand, you should try some of the new styles that come out each year.

When I began painting, starter kits had three brushes: a no. 1 liner, a no. 6 flat and a no. 5 round. How things have changed! I used Loew-Cornell brushes (pictured to the right) for this book, but not every brush is used for every project. Specific brush needs are listed at the beginning of each project.

In addition to brushes used to paint the borders, I recommend keeping a few 1-inch (25mm) washes or disposable foam brushes on hand. I use one exclusively for sealing, another for basecoating and a third for varnishing.

Brush Basin

Loew-Cornell has a brush basin that has ridges in the bottom to help clean paint from the brush between color changes. But if you choose, there's nothing wrong with using an empty cottage cheese container or something similar.

Loew-Cornell Brushes
(left to right) liner, series 7350C; script liner, series 7050; shader, series 7300; angular, series 7400; stroke, series 7100; wash, series 7550; filbert, series 7500; round, series 7000; round stroke, series 7040; disposable foam; spotter, series 3650.

Palette

Of the many types available, I recommend a waxed palette for acrylics. Masterson's Sta-Wet palette keeps paint usable for a long time and is readily available at hobby and painting stores.

I've also found that a shallow school pencil box can make a great palette with the help of deli paper and a paper towel. I use an interfolded deli paper called Kabinet Wax Deli Wrap, put out by Dixie.

1 Arrange Papers
Take a paper towel square, fold it in half and place it inside the deli paper. Fold the deli paper over the towel and trim all layers to fit the pencil box.

2 Place Papers in Box and Add Water
Place the deli paper and paper towel in the pencil box. Lift the top layer of the deli paper and pour water on the paper towel to dampen. Don't get the towel too wet, or it will dilute the paint.

3 Slip Back the Deli Paper
Fold the top layer of deli paper back over the dampened towel and smooth it out.

4 Redampen When Necessary
If the towel dries out while you're painting, just lift a corner of the deli paper and redampen the paper towel with a spritz from a water bottle.

Additional Supplies

Round out your painting supplies with these commonly used items.

1 Delta All-Purpose Sealer
This product is used to seal the grain of wood so it's not so porous. Be sure you seal all surfaces, inside and outside, so the wood doesn't warp. Some people sand the wood before sealing and then sand again, but I've found that sealing the wood first and then sanding works just as well and eliminates the need to sand twice.

2 Sanding pads
These little ovals come in four different grits. When I recommend sanding between coats, use the very fine grit.

3 Tack cloth
This is cheese cloth with a varnish medium applied to make dust and lint stick to it. I highly recommend wiping your surface with this cloth after sanding and before varnishing.

4 Tracing paper
Use this translucent paper to trace original patterns, make surface templates and design borders.

5 Chalk pencil These pencils come in many colors. I use them when I'm designing a border right on the painting surface. Sharpened school chalk also works well.

6 Super Chacopaper
This is my preferred transfer paper. As the name suggests, transfer paper is used to transfer a traced pattern onto a painting surface. Chacopaper lines can later be removed by patting them with a water-dampened paper towel. I've even removed lines under paint.

7 White and gray graphite paper
This is another type of transfer paper. Removing excess lines made with this paper requires an eraser.

8 Paper towels
Paper towels have a variety of uses in painting. I use them in my homemade palette (see page 7).

They're also handy for soaking up excess moisture on your brush, cleaning up stray paint or mediums and removing Chacopaper lines. Use the most lint-free towels you can find. Blue shop towels or Bounty are good choices.

9 Pencil and eraser
Keep a pencil on hand for a variety of tasks—designing borders, taking notes and filling in pattern lines. For corrections or cleanup, I recommend an art gum or a plastic eraser, such as Staedtler Mars Plastic. These are gentle on paint and leave little residue.

10 Stylus
This versatile tool has several uses. When used to transfer patterns, it gives you cleaner, clearer lines than a pencil or pen. You can also use it for applying embossed stenciling and for making paint dots. I use a double-ended stylus with two different sizes of ball ends. The smaller ball makes smaller dots and fits into smaller areas of an embossing stencil.

11 Mini paint roller and pan
This is a handy tool for preparing larger surfaces. The roller gives good coverage without the ridges a brush tends to create.

12 Painter's tape
This is used for masking or for keeping patterns or stencils in place. Blue masking tape, Kleen Edge tape and invisible cellophane tape are all good. Use any tape that sticks to the surface, won't allow paint to seep underneath and comes off easily without removing the basecoat.

13 T square
This is so much handier than a plain ruler when working with borders. I use the C-Thru Junior T-square, JR-12.

14 Delta Exterior/Interior Varnish
As the name suggests, this product protects a surface indoors and outdoors. It comes in both gloss and satin finishes. You can also apply a light coat of finishing wax over the varnish to protect the surface from water damage.

Chapter 2 Techniques

These next few pages can save you frustration as you paint the projects in this book or design your own borders. If you're new to decorative painting, the sections on brush loads and making dots will get you started on the right foot. The next sections teach the basics of border building and project designing.

Loading the Brush

Loading a Round or Liner

Roll the liner or round as you pull it from the side of a paint puddle. This maintains the brush point and allows an even, full load.

Loading an Angular, Shader or Filbert

1 Dip one surface of the brush into the paint puddle and pull out. Flip the brush and load the other surface. Blend on the palette.

2 Here is the loaded brush. This even loading helps you avoid ridges when you paint.

Side Loading an Angular, Shader or Filbert

Dampen the brush with water and pull one side of the brush through the side of the paint puddle. Note that one side of the brush remains free of paint.

Side Loading a Round or Liner

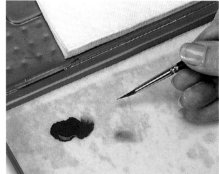

1 You can also side load a round or liner brush. First flatten the dampened bristles with your fingers or by stroking on your palette.

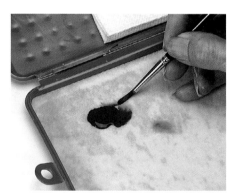

2 Then pull one side of the brush through the side of the paint puddle as you would do with an angular, shader or filbert.

Loading the Brush *(continued)*
Double Loading an Angular, Shader or Filbert

1 Double loading involves two paint colors. First pull one brush corner into the first paint color.

2 Then pull the opposite corner into the second paint color.

3 Blend the colors on your palette by stroking the brush a few times. This creates a new value.

Making Dots
Brush Handle Dots

1 To make brush handle dots, dip just the tip into a paint puddle. The larger the handle tip, the larger the dots.

2 This is the proper amount of paint on a freshly loaded brush handle.

For very small dots, use a stylus tip. A double-tipped stylus gives you two choices of dot size.

Uniform, Random and Diminishing Dots

Always make dots with fresh paint—it's much easier to work with than paint that's been sitting out for hours.

a. Make uniformly sized dots by reloading for each dot.

b. Make randomly sized dots by reloading every third or fourth dot.

c. Make diminishing dots by continuing to make dots without reloading.

a   b   c

Building a Border

You can create a border with just a few simple tools—something to draw with, something to draw on and something to keep your lines straight. A T square is an excellent tool for drawing straight parallel lines. Graph paper also helps you keep straight lines, not to mention maintain consistent spacing. A pencil is fine for designing on paper. (Keep a good artist eraser handy!) If you're designing on your actual painting surface, I recommend a chalk pencil.

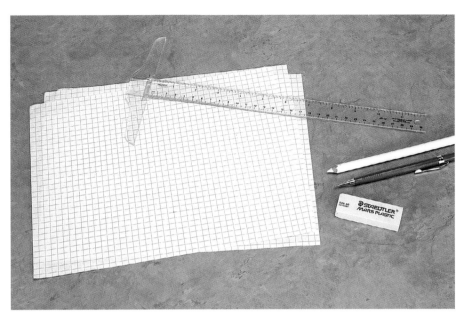

1 Draw Boundary Lines
Draw dashed lines to establish the upper and lower border boundaries.

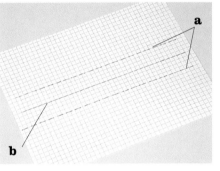

2 Draw Spine Line
Halfway between the boundaries (a), draw a solid line. This solid line is called the "spine" (b).

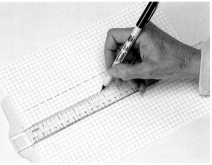

3 Mark Sections
Borders have repeating sections, generally of the same length. Mark the lengths of the sections.

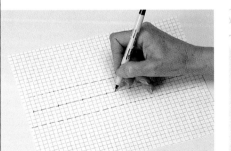

4 Mark Helper Dots
Borders are often based on a scroll, such as a C-stroke scroll. Helper dots establish where you will begin each section's scroll.

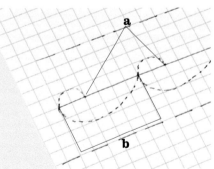

5 Begin Border Design
Note how these C-stroke scrolls begin at the helper dots (a) and fill the space between the section markings (b). From this start you can build up embellishments such as strokes, dots, linework or even pictorial elements. Just be sure the border stays within the upper and lower boundary lines.

Scrolls and Lifelines

Many borders are based on scrolls, such as the C-stroke scroll on page 12, or on a lifeline. Below are a few examples of good starting elements for borders. From these simple starts, you can add any number of embellishments.

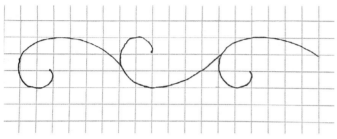

Alternating C-stroke Scrolls

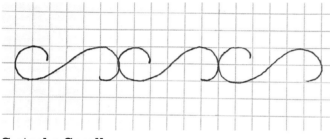

S-stroke Scrolls

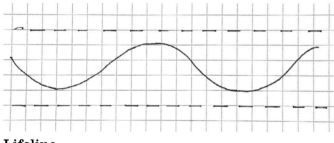

Lifeline

Adding Embellishments

Building . . .

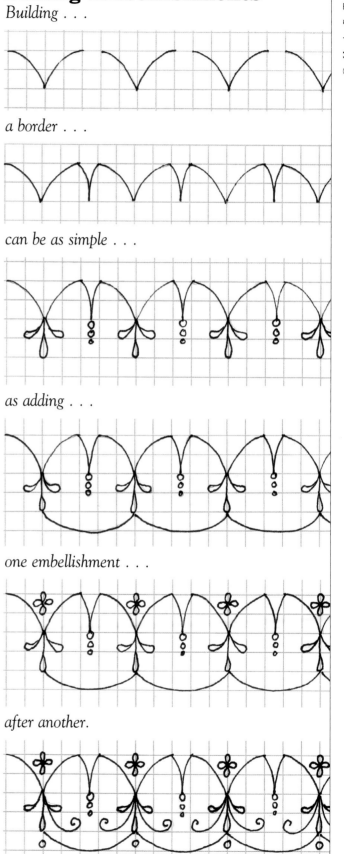

a border . . .

can be as simple . . .

as adding . . .

one embellishment . . .

after another.

Designing a Project

Building a border is just one part of designing a project that includes borders. You also have to know how your border will fit the surface. Because borders are created with repeating motifs, you can simplify your designing by drawing a portion of the border and then retracing it on folded tissue paper. The demonstration below shows this fold-and-trace designing technique for a project on a square surface. Using the same principles, you can design for surfaces of other shapes and sizes.

1 Cut and Fold a Tissue Template
Cut a sheet of tissue paper the same size as your project surface. Then fold the tissue in half horizontally and vertically and on both diagonals. Draw pencil lines along the folds to make them easier to see.

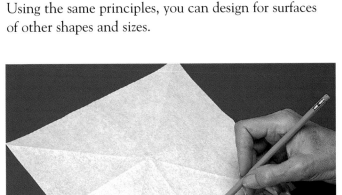

2 Mark Boundary and Spine Lines
Turn the tissue over and mark your boundary lines and spine across one of the triangular quarters. Working from diagonal line to diagonal line lets you work out the corners of your design.

Template Tip

You can create a surface template without measuring. Just lay your tissue paper over the surface and rub the side of a pencil over the tissue at the surface edges. The edges of your pencil shading will exactly match the perimeter of your surface. Using this method, you know for sure your pattern will fit.

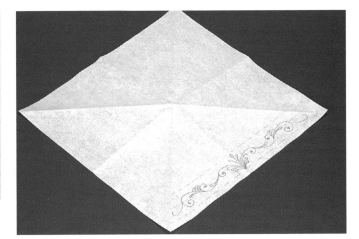

3 Draw Border on the First Quarter
Draw your border. You can use a border previously designed or you can design as you draw.

4 **Trace Border on the Second Quarter**
Fold the tissue on a diagonal and trace the design on the second quarter. Be sure all your folds line up.

5 **Trace Border on the Third Quarter**
Open the tissue and fold it again so you can trace the third quarter.

6 **Trace the Border on the Fourth Quarter**
Open the tissue and fold it so you can trace the fourth quarter.

7 **Unfold Completed Pattern**
You now have the design around the perimeter of the tissue, which you can use as a transfer pattern. Since the tissue was sized to your project, you know the design will fit just right.

Letter *Rack*

S urfaces for decorative painting are available everywhere—not just in your local hobby shop. I bought this ready-made letter rack in a national chain discount store. It opens to a narrow space with hooks for hanging keys. Kitchen departments are a great source for project pieces.

Keep this in mind when you're buying gifts. The addition of a simple handpainted border adds a personal touch your friend or loved one is certain to appreciate.

Painting preparation for a prefinished surface differs from that of an unfinished surface. You don't necessarily have to sand the entire piece—just make sure the area where you intend to paint is dulled by sanding so the paint will adhere.

Materials

Surface

- Hardwood letter rack with key holder, no. 1475W (Available at Wal-Mart)

Paint Delta Ceramcoat Acrylics

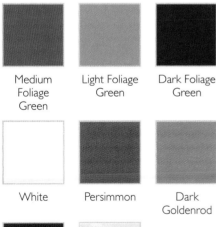

| Medium Foliage Green | Light Foliage Green | Dark Foliage Green |
| White | Persimmon | Dark Goldenrod |

Burnt Sienna

Mello Yellow

Loew-Cornell Brushes

- No. 18/0 script liner, series 7050
- No. 5 round, series 7000
- ¼-inch (6mm) angular, series 7400
- No. 2 filbert, series 7500
- 1-inch (25mm) wash, series 7550, or disposable foam brush for varnishing

Additional Supplies

- Sanding pad
- Tack cloth or damp paper towel
- Tracing paper and pencil
- White Super Chacopaper
- Stylus
- Delta Exterior/Interior Satin Varnish

See pages 134 and 135 for patterns.

Using a Ready-made, *Finished Surface*

1 Prepare to Paint
Lightly sand the front and side areas of the letter rack that will have the design. The shiny surface needs to be dulled down by sanding in order for the paint to adhere. Wipe off the dust with a tack cloth or damp paper towel. Trace the design and transfer it to the front and sides of the rack.

2 Base Large Leaves
Load a ¼-inch (6mm) angular brush with Medium Foliage Green. Tip the toe with Light Foliage Green and fill in the large leaves, using a back-and-forth sliding motion to create veining.

3 Shade Large Leaves
Let the leaves dry. Then, using the same brush, side load the toe in Dark Foliage Green only and pull shading down the leaf centers.

4 Paint Thin Stems
The thin stems are lifelines painted with the no. 18/0 script liner and Light, Medium and Dark Foliage Green. Paint each color separately, letting the different colored lifelines intertwine with each other.

5 Add Filler Leaves and Large Stems
Paint the small filler leaves with one stroke of Light Foliage Green and the no. 2 filbert. You can add leaves that aren't on the pattern to give a more casual look. Paint the larger stems with Dark Foliage Green on the no. 18/0 script liner.

6 Paint Petals

Add a bit of White to Persimmon and paint in the back flower petals using a no. 5 round. Reload the brush in Persimmon, tip in White and stroke in the remaining petals, adding more White to the petal tips toward the front.

7 Paint Flower Centers

Load the no. 2 filbert with Dark Goldenrod and base in the centers. Shade the part of the flower petals closest to the flower centers with a side load of Persimmon. Shade the flower centers with Burnt Sienna. Tap in a highlight with Mello Yellow. This shading and highlighting helps create the button in the middle of the flower center.

8 Add Stamens

Dot in the stamens with Mello Yellow on a stylus. Let dry. Remove the transfer lines and then varnish.

Front

Side

Clock

Round surfaces aren't generally a challenge in painting borders when you're working with a premade pattern. Just be sure you line up the pattern correctly so the design doesn't appear off-center. Take special care when you have only a partial pattern for a repeating border design, such as is used for the clock frame in this project. As you reposition the pattern, be sure you overlap already traced areas, exactly lining up the pattern design with the traced design. Keep these principles in mind and you'll do fine.

Designing a pattern for a round surface can be challenging. Here's where the fold-and-trace method described under "Designing a Project" (pages 14-15) really comes in handy.

Materials

Surface

- 15" (38cm) diameter clock, Stan Brown Arts & Crafts # 97-01410

Paint *Delta Ceramcoat Acrylics*

Trail Tan   Putty   Sea Grass

Rosetta Pink   Coral   Butter Cream

Pale Yellow

Loew-Cornell Brushes

- No. 10/0 script liner, series 7050
- No. 4 round, series 7000
- ¼-inch (6mm) angular, series 7400
- ½-inch (13mm) angular, series 7400
- No. 2 filbert, series 7500
- 1-inch (25mm) wash, series 7550, or disposable foam brushes for sealing, basing and varnishing (See "Brushes," page 6.)

Additional Supplies

- Tracing paper and pencil
- Delta All-Purpose Sealer
- Sanding pad
- Tack cloth or damp paper towel
- Blue Super Chacopaper
- Stylus
- Delta Exterior/Interior Satin Varnish
- Clockworks (The clock surface I used for this project comes with clockworks, but if you use a different surface, you may need separate clockworks.)

See page 135 for patterns.

Border on *Round Surface*

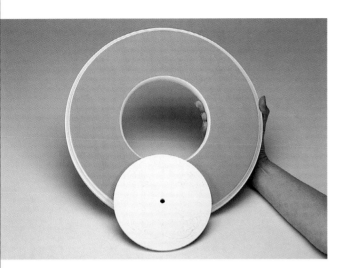

1 Prepare Surface, Base and Transfer Design

Trace the design and set aside. Seal the frame and the clock face—front and back—with All-Purpose Sealer. Let dry and then sand. Remove sanding dust with a tack cloth or damp paper towel. Basecoat the top only of the frame with two coats of Trail Tan, sanding lightly between coats. Base the clock face and the routed outside edge of the frame with Putty. Sand lightly to make sure the surfaces are smooth. Remove the sanding dust. Transfer the design with blue Chacopaper. You'll need to reposition the frame pattern a few times, overlapping already traced areas.

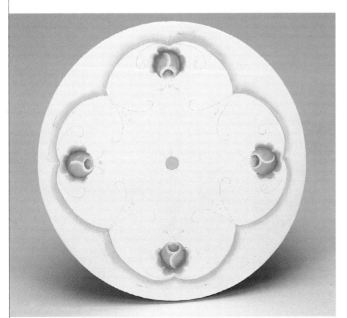

2 Paint Outer Linework on Clock Face

Paint outside the curved linework on the outer edge of the clock face design with Sea Grass side loaded on a ½-inch (13mm) angular brush.

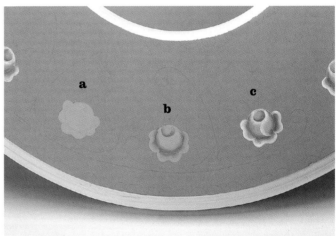

3 Paint the Roses

The frame and the clock face have the same rose border. Refer to the photos above and to the left.

a. Basecoat the roses with Rosetta Pink and a no. 2 filbert. You may need to apply two coats.

b. Using the same brush, shade with a side load of Coral around the base of the ball of the rose, inside the throat and on the petals, next to the ball.

c. Still using the same brush, highlight the outside edges of the petals around the top and across the face of the ball with a side load of Butter Cream.

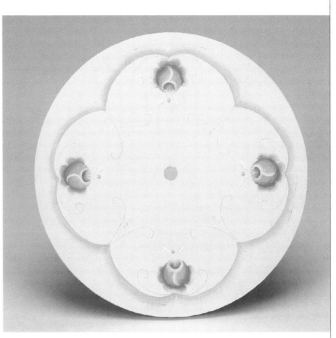

4 Paint Stamens

Paint the stamens with strokes of Pale Yellow and a no. 10/0 script liner. Use a stylus to place a dot of Sea Grass between the stamens.

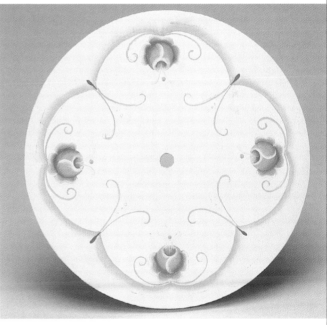

5 Paint Linework and Strokes

Paint the linework on both surfaces with a no. 10/0 script liner and thinned Sea Grass. Paint the stroke at the base of the hooked lines with Coral, using a no. 4 round.

Border on *Round Surface*

6 Add Scalloped Borders

With a side load of Sea Grass on the ¼-inch (6mm) angular brush, add small scallops around the inner and outer edges of the frame. Keep them uniform in length and width.

7 Add Small Stroke Border

Paint the small stroke border on the outer frame with Pale Yellow and the no. 10/0 script liner.

8 Add Dots

All dots on both the frame and the face are painted with a stylus. Start with the dots closest to the center and work your way out. Use Coral for the dots between the inner scallops on the frame. Use Butter Cream to paint the diminishing dots (see page 11) between the large hooked scrolls on both surfaces. Dot Pale Yellow at the point of the Coral strokes and at the base of the roses. On the frame, paint the elongated dot connecting the curved linework between the roses with Butter Cream by moving the stylus back and forth. Use Rosetta Pink to paint the dots between the outer scallops on the frame

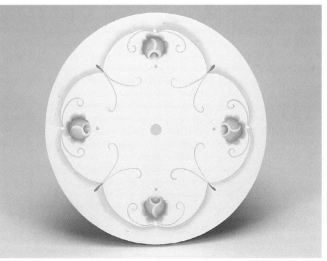

Transfer Line Tip

Transfer lines made with Chacopaper can be removed with a damp paper towel. Transfer lines made with graphite paper can be removed with an art eraser.

9 Varnish

Let dry. Remove visible transfer lines and then varnish. Install the clockworks according to package directions.

Lazy Susan *&* Place Mat

hese projects remind me of a Dutch Delft painting. They use only two colors, one for the background and one for the design. Reversing these colors, as I did from the lazy Susan to the place mats, creates a pleasing coordinated effect. If blue doesn't fit your décor, you can substitute another color for an easy adjustment.

Here you can see that strokes and linework alone can make not only an elegant border but an entire design. You'll find several examples of this type of border on pages 72-73 in "Three-Step Borders" and also scattered throughout the "Hundreds of Borders" section.

Because of the combination of the rounded surfaces and the intricate border patterns used for these projects, you need to take special care to line up the patterns correctly and to transfer the designs accurately.

Materials

Surfaces

- 15¾" (40cm) diameter lazy Susan, Wildwood #LS-100
- 17" × 13½" (43cm × 34cm) oval Kreative Kanvas by Kunin Felt

Paint *Delta Ceramcoat Acrylics*

■	□
Opaque Blue	White

Loew-Cornell Brushes

- No. 0 liner, series 7350C
- ½-inch (13mm) stroke, series 7100
- No. 2 round stroke, series 7040
- 1-inch (25mm) wash or disposable foam brushes for sealing, basing and varnishing the lazy Susan only (See "Brushes," page 6.)

Additional Supplies

Needed for lazy Susan and place mat
- Sanding pad
- Tack cloth or damp paper towel
- Tracing paper and pencil
- Delta Ceramcoat Acrylic Thinner
- Stylus
- Delta Exterior/Interior Satin Varnish

Needed for lazy Susan only
- Delta All-Purpose Sealer
- White Super Chacopaper
- Felt (optional—see step 5)

Needed for place mat only
- Gesso
- Mini roller and pan
- Blue Super Chacopaper

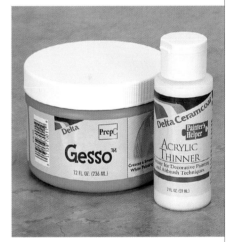

Specialized Supplies
Gesso and acrylic thinner are specialized but easy-to-find supplies. The acrylic thinner is used on both the lazy Susan and the place mat. The gesso is used only on the place mat.

See pages 134 and 135 for patterns.

Lazy Susan

1 **Prepare Surface, Base, and Trace Design**
Remove the base from the top. Seal the surfaces with All-Purpose Sealer and then sand. Remove sanding dust with a tack cloth or damp paper towel. Basecoat both pieces with two coats of Opaque Blue. Paint the outside edge of the top in White, using a ½-inch (13mm) stroke brush. Trace the design and then transfer it onto the surface. You'll need to reposition the pattern a few times, overlapping already traced areas. Be sure you accurately transfer the curves and lengths of the fanned strokes in the middle and the outside border, or your painted design will lose its balance and precision.

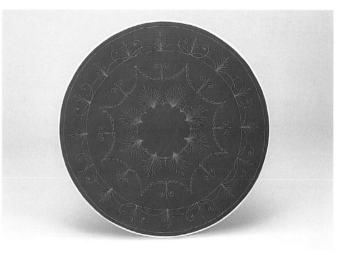

2 **Paint Linework**
Paint the entire design with White. To avoid paint smears, always work from the inside out. First establish the linework of the design with a no. 0 liner. Thin the paint for this with Delta Ceramcoat Acrylic Thinner. For the innermost scalloped lines (a), start each scallop on the brush tip, press down as you approach the middle of the scallop and then lift as you approach the end. This gives the thin-to-thick-to-thin appearance.

3 **Add Strokes**
Now paint the strokes, starting from the inside and working out. Use a no. 2 round stroke brush without thinner.

Basecoating Tip

To keep a smooth delineation between basecoat colors, make long sweeps as you basecoat the White edges, holding the side of your brush against the top or bottom of the surface edge.

4 Place the Dots
Paint the big dots with a brush handle. Use a stylus for small dots and diminishing dots (see page 11).

5 Paint the Outer Border
The outside border consists of small strokes. Paint them with a no. 0 liner and let dry. Remove the transfer lines and then varnish. You may wish to apply protective felt to the bottom of the base.

Place Mat

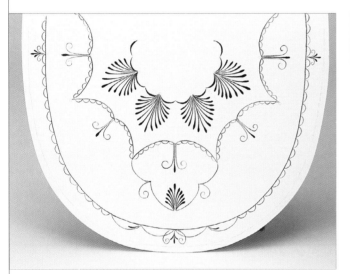

1 Prepare Surface, Base and Paint Linework
Using a small paint roller and roller pan, apply one coat of gesso to the front and back of the place mat to seal. Let dry and then sand lightly. Remove the sanding dust with a tack cloth or damp paper towel and then roll two coats of White on the side you'll use to paint the design. Sand if necessary and remove the dust. Trace the design and then transfer with blue Chacopaper.

Paint the entire design with Opaque Blue. To avoid paint smears, always work from the inside out. First establish the linework of the design with a no. 0 liner. Thin the paint for this with Delta Ceramcoat Acrylic Thinner.

To paint the innermost scallops, start on the brush tip, press down as you approach the middle of the scallop and then lift as you approach the end. This gives the line a thin-to-thick-to-thin appearance.

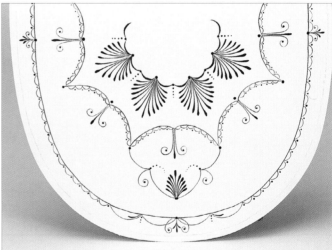

2 Add Strokes
Now paint the strokes, starting from the inside and working out. Use a no. 2 round stroke brush without thinner.

3 Place Dots
Paint the big dots with a brush handle. Use a stylus to paint the small dots and diminishing dots (see page 11).

Dotting Tip
When doing dots, fresh paint is much easier to work with than paint that has been on the palette for a day or so.

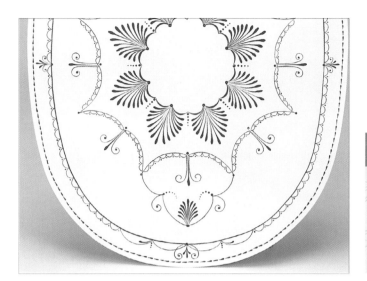

Line Pulling Tip

When you run out of paint in the middle of a line, reload and resume your linework in front of where you ran out, blending the two sections as you pull the brush toward you. This keeps the line smooth.

4 Paint the Outer Border
The outside border consists of small strokes. Paint them with a no. 0 liner and let dry. Remove the transfer lines and then varnish.

Strawbaby *Pie Basket*

i like to put a little fun into my painting. When I was designing this piece, a devilish streak within me made me give the berries faces. I thought the hulls looked like hats, and I went on from there.

Sometimes a border is all a project needs, but often, as with this picnic basket, the border alone leaves a space in the middle that begs to be filled. Generally you can lift a motif from your border for a central design. For this project I used two variations of the strawberry motif, one on the lid and the other on the inner tray.

Materials

Surface

- 8" x 13" x 13" (20mm x 33mm x 33mm) pie basket with 10" x 10" (25mm x 25mm) inner tray, Stan Brown Arts & Crafts #97-10011

Loew-Cornell Brushes

- No. 0 liner, series 7350C
- No. 2 round stroke, series 7040
- ¼-inch (6mm) angular, series 7400
- No. 4 filbert, series 7500
- 1-inch (25mm) wash or disposable foam brushes for sealing, basing and varnishing (See "Brushes," page 6.)

Additional Supplies

- Delta All-Purpose Sealer
- Sanding pad
- Tack cloth or damp paper towel
- Tracing paper and pencil
- Blue Super Chacopaper
- Stylus
- Delta Exterior/Interior Satin Varnish

Paint Delta Ceramcoat Acrylics

Candlelight	Medium Foliage Green	Black
Dark Foliage Green	Light Foliage Green	Crimson
Rooster Red	Napthol Red Light	White
Crocus Yellow		

See page 136 for patterns.

Border with *Centered Border Motif*

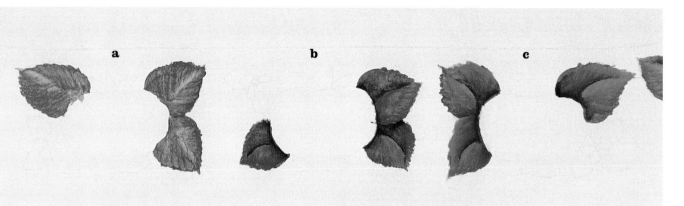

1 Prepare Surface, Base and Transfer Design

Seal and sand the lid, tops of the handles and the inner tray. Remove sanding dust with a tack cloth or damp paper towel. Basecoat these surfaces with two coats of Candlelight, sanding lightly between coats. Remember to remove the sanding dust. Trace the design onto tracing paper. Transfer the design to the lid and the inner tray, using blue Super Chacopaper. Leave off the face details at this time.

2 Base, Shade and Highlight Large Leaves

The lid border, lid center and inner tray are basically the same design. These directions are based on the lid border, with instructions for the differences on the lid center and the inner tray in steps 10 and 11.

a. Basecoat the large leaves behind the strawberries with Medium Foliage Green on a ¼-inch (6mm) angular. Slide the brush back and forth to create veins. Let dry.

b. Mix a touch of Black into Dark Foliage Green. Side load the ¼-inch (6mm) angular and shade between the leaves, under the strawberries and down the middle of the leaves.

c. Side load the same brush with Light Foliage Green and highlight the center of the leaves and some of the outside edges.

3 Stroke in Blossom Leaves

Stroke in the small blossom leaves with Dark Foliage Green on a no. 2 round stroke, painting carefully around the blossom petals.

4 Base and Shade Strawberries, Transfer Faces

a. Base the strawberries with Crimson on a no. 4 filbert. Use two coats.

b. Using the same brush, shade the edges of the strawberries with a side load of Rooster Red.

c. Let dry and then transfer the face details.

5 Paint Strawberry Faces

Paint the cheeks, nose and lower lip with a ¼-inch (6mm) angular side-loaded with Napthol Red Light. Paint the eyes with Black on a no. 2 round stroke. Let dry and then shade around the eyes and behind the nose with a side load of Rooster Red, using the ¼-inch (6mm) angular brush. Highlight the eyes with a dot and a curved line of White. Outline the nose and paint the mouth with a no. 0 liner and Rooster Red. Add the tiny dot highlights to the nose and mouth with White on the very tip of the liner.

6 Add Leaf Caps

Paint the leaf caps on top of the strawberries with Light, Medium and Dark Foliage Green, loaded together on the no. 2 round stroke.

7 Paint Blossoms and Dot Seeds

Using White on the no. 2 round stroke, paint the blossom petals. Dot in the blossom centers with Crocus Yellow and a stylus. Still using the stylus, dot in the strawberry seeds with Rooster Red, staying out of the face area.

8 Pull Tendrils, Dash in Border

Using Light Foliage Green on the no. 0 liner, pull freehand tendrils connecting the berries. Paint the dashed border with Light Foliage Green, using the same brush.

Border with *Centered Border Motif*

9 Dash in Handle Lines

At this time you can also paint the dashed lines down the center of the handles.

10 Paint Center Strawberry on Lid

Paint the strawberry design in the center of the lid using the same colors, brushes and techniques as were used for the lid border berries. The leaf and strawberry stems are painted in Dark Foliage Green with a no. 0 liner.

11 Paint Strawberry on Inner Tray

The inner tray design is painted with the same colors as the lid design. You can also use the same brushes, just applying more pressure to make up for the larger size of the design. The technique varies only in the following areas:

Blossoms The petals are painted with two strokes. Once dry, side load a ¼-inch (6mm) angular with Light Foliage Green and tap in shading around the center. Complete the blossom by tapping in a Crocus Yellow center with a stylus.

Blossom Leaves Use a side-loaded ¼-inch (6mm) angular to highlight the centers of these leaves.

Eyes Use a no. 0 liner brush to place a wedge of White beside the Black of the open eye. Add a white highlight. Using a side load of Rooster Red on the ¼-inch (6mm) angular, place a crescent of shading along the top of the closed eyelid. With the no. 0 liner add Black eyelashes to both eyes.

Dashed Border Use Light Foliage Green on the no. 0 liner to paint the dashed border as you did on the lid and handles, but leave spaces for Crimson stylus dots between the dashes. Once the paint is dry, remove the transfer lines and then varnish.

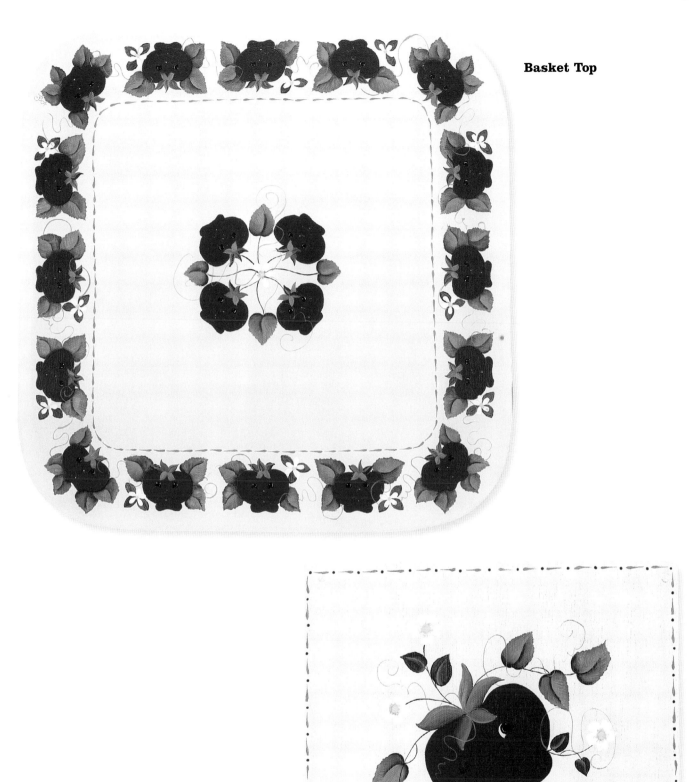

Basket Top

Inner Tray

Pillowcase

Wouldn't this pillowcase make a nice housewarming or shower gift! You could even paint a matching top sheet to create a coordinated bed linen set.

Painting on fabric requires a couple of simple adjustments. First, you need to devise a way to keep your fabric taut. I recommend taping the fabric in place across a piece of stiff cardboard. Second, you need to use the proper paint or paint medium. Paint especially formulated for fabrics exists, but in this project I use ordinary acrylics. The key is to mix each of your paint colors with textile medium.

Now that you know the secrets, think of all the border projects you could paint on fabric—tablecloths, napkins, place mats, shirt cuffs and collars, bookmarks. The list goes on and on.

Materials

Surface
- White standard size pillowcase

Paint *Delta Ceramcoat Acrylics*

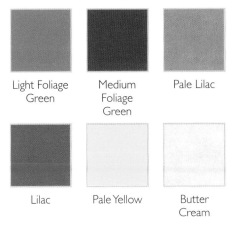

Light Foliage Green   Medium Foliage Green   Pale Lilac

Lilac   Pale Yellow   Butter Cream

Loew-Cornell Brushes
- No. 10/0 liner, series 7350C
- No. 4 filbert, series 7500

Additional Supplies
- Tracing paper
- Extra-fine point permanent ink marker
- Ruler or tape measure
- Water erasable fabric marker
- Stiff cardboard, 8½" x 19½" (21.6cm x 49.5cm) or width of pillowcase
- Plastic wrap
- Masking tape
- Delta Ceramcoat Painter's Helper Textile Medium
- Ribbon and lace trim of choice
- Soft cloth and iron
- White thread
- Needle or sewing machine

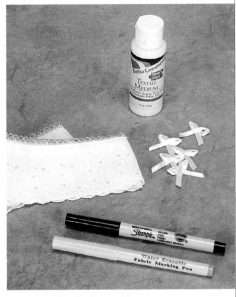

Specialized Supplies
Textile medium, lace trim, ribbon, an extra-fine point permanent ink marker and a water erasable fabric marker are specialized but easy-to-find supplies used for this project.

See page 137 for patterns.

1 Prepare Pillowcase

Prewash, dry and iron the pillowcase. Don't use fabric softener or dryer sheets. Trace the design onto tracing paper with an extra-fine point permanent ink marker. The tracing must be dark enough to be seen through the fabric. Set it aside to dry. Measure 1" (25mm) up from the pillowcase bottom hem and, using a water erasable fabric marker, make a solid line from one side of the case to the other. Mark off 2½" (6.4cm) increments on the solid line.

2 Transfer the pattern

Tightly wrap an 8½" x 19½" (21.6cm x 49.5cm) piece of stiff cardboard in plastic wrap. Slide the cardboard into the case. Then slide the traced pattern between the cardboard and the fabric. Make sure the case is pulled smooth over the cardboard. Align the pattern so the daisy stems fall on the 2½" (6.4cm) markings. Transfer the pattern with a water erasable fabric marker. (Don't use an air erasable pen, or the transferred design will disappear before you get it painted.) You may need to adjust the spacing a bit.

3 Tape Case, Base and Shade Leaves

Remove the pattern and tape the case tautly to the cardboard so the fabric won't crawl as you're painting. Be sure you tape the excess fabric out of the way to the back of the cardboard. Since you're using regular acrylic paint rather than textile paint, you must brush mix all your paint with textile medium. When changing colors, wipe the excess paint from the brush and clean the color out with textile medium. DO NOT rinse the brush in water, or the paint will bleed into the fabric. If you must use water, blot the brush extremely well.

Base the leaves with Light Foliage Green and a no. 4 filbert. Side load the filbert with Medium Foliage Green to shade the center line.

4 Paint Daisies, Highlight Leaves

With the same brush, paint the daisy petals with Pale Lilac. Use a no. 10/0 liner to paint Lilac gathering lines at the base of the petals. Base the daisy centers with Pale Yellow on a no. 4 filbert. Then tap in Light Foliage Green at the bottom for shading. Highlight the flower centers and the leaves with a side load of Butter Cream.

Laundering Tip

Because you've mixed your paint with textile medium, the painted pillowcase may be laundered normally.

5 Paint Stems, Strokes and Scallops

The stems and green strokes are painted with a no. 10/0 liner. Stems and hook strokes are Light Foliage Green. The large strokes are Medium Foliage Green.

Still using the no. 10/0 liner, paint the scallops under the daisies with Pale Lilac. The strokes at the points are Lilac.

6 Sew on Trim

Let the paint dry 24 to 48 hours and then remove the tracing lines with a damp paper towel. Place a soft cloth over the design and heat set with an iron.

For a neat finish on the lace trim, open the side seam so you can tuck in the lace edges. Pin the lace in place and sew it down. Then re-sew the side seam. Tie small ribbon bows and sew them on the lace at the base of the stems.

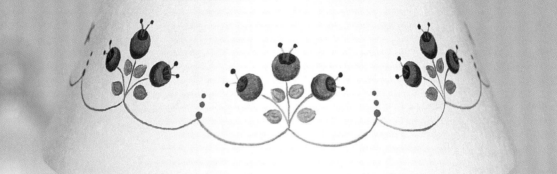

Flowerpot Candle Holder *with Shade*

When I designed this project, I imagined a row of these candle holders down the center of a picnic table. At night you could use anti-mosquito candles in place of tea lights. But you don't have to paint a whole row. Even one of these candle holders adds a charming touch, and it could be a cute, easy-to-make hostess gift.

Curved surfaces may require an unusually shaped pattern—one you might not be able to figure out by just looking at the object. For example, both the flowerpot and shade patterns for this project look like segments of a ring. This is no problem when you're working with a premade pattern, but it might seem daunting if you're designing a pattern for a curved surface. Simplify this process by making a template of your surface out of tissue paper. Bend the tissue around the curves and mark the edges of the painting surface on your tissue. You may need to snip the paper so it can lie flat to the surface. Cut out the tissue on your outline and wrap it around your surface again to check the fit. Make adjustments as necessary. When you're satisfied with the fit, you can design your border right on the tissue paper template.

Materials

Surfaces

- 4" (10cm) clay flowerpot and saucer, available from craft store or garden center
- Wall-Liner for Borders, 6¹¹/₁₆" (17cm), no. ALLB6 from Eisenhart Wallcovering Co., sold only through Sherwin-Williams

Paint *Delta Ceramcoat Acrylics*

Medium Foliage Green   Wild Rose   Black Cherry

Light Ivory   White

Delta Air-Dry PermEnamel

Victorian Rose   **See page 134 for patterns.**

Loew-Cornell Brushes

- No. 0 liner, series 7350C
- No. 0 round, series 7000
- No. 4 shader, series 7300
- 1-inch (25mm) wash, series 7550, or disposable foam brushes for conditioner, varnish and gesso (see "Brushes," page 6.)

Additional Supplies

- Sanding pad
- Paper towels
- Delta Air-Dry PermEnamel Surface Conditioner
- Stencil sponge
- Tracing paper and pencil
- White and blue Super Chaco paper
- Ruler
- Chalk pencil
- Stylus
- Delta CeramDecor Air-Dry Perm Enamel Clear Gloss Glaze
- Gesso

- Delta Exterior/Interior Satin Varnish or Delta Stencil Magic top coat Satin Spray
- Scissors
- Delta Quick 'n Tacky Glue
- Tea light candle

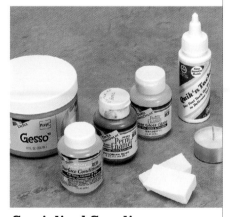

Specialized Supplies

Gesso, PermEnamel Surface Conditioner, PermEnamel paint, PermEnamel Clear Gloss Glaze, Quik 'n Glue, stencil sponges and tea lights are specialized but easy-to-find supplies used for this project.

Tracing Tip

Since flower pots vary, you may want to get a tissue template of your pot before tracing the pattern. Then you can make any necessary adjustments as you trace the pattern onto your custom-sized tissue.

2 Paint Leaves, Stems and Linework

Paint the leaves, stems and scalloped lines in Medium Foliage Green. Use a no. 0 round for the leaves and a no. 0 liner for the stems and lines.

3 Paint Roses

Using a no. 4 shader, base the roses in Wild Rose and shade them with a side load of Black Cherry.

1 Prepare Pot and Saucer

Sand any rough edges from the pot and saucer. Wash and dry well. Apply Delta Air-Dry Perm-Enamel Surface Conditioner to the pot and saucer, using a stencil sponge. With a clean stencil sponge, base with Victorian Rose PermEnamel in a patting motion. Trace the pattern and transfer with white Chacopaper.

To transfer the pattern onto the saucer, first mark off 1" (25mm) increments with a chalk pencil. Line up one of the large roses (with stem) from the pot pattern on a chalk mark and transfer. Reposition and continue around the saucer. Note that the saucer is turned upside down.

4 Apply Dots

Apply the dots with Light Ivory and a stylus.

Warning!

Even though the paper shade is far enough from the flame to be safe under normal conditions, you should never let a candle burn unattended.

5 Sponge Saucer Rim, Varnish

With a stencil sponge, pat White on the rim of the saucer. When the pot and saucer are dry, remove the tracing lines with a damp paper towel. Then varnish with clear gloss glaze.

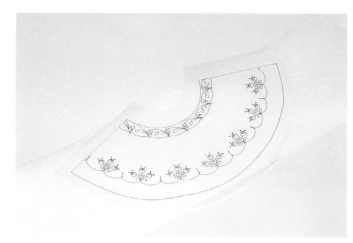

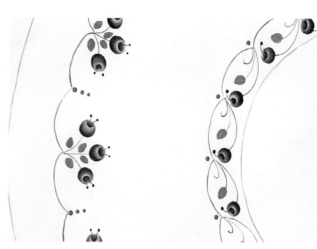

6 Prepare Shade

Trace the pattern and position it onto wall-liner paper. When positioned correctly, the pattern will just fit on the border paper, as you see in the photograph. Transfer only the shade outline. Base the shade with gesso. Dry well. Then transfer the design with blue Chacopaper and a stylus.

7 Paint Shade

Paint the shade using the same colors and brushes as you did for the flowerpot in steps 2 and 3. Then add stamen stems in Medium Foliage Green, painted with a no. 0 liner. Stamen dots are painted with a stylus in Black Cherry. Diminishing dots (see page 11) are Wild Rose.

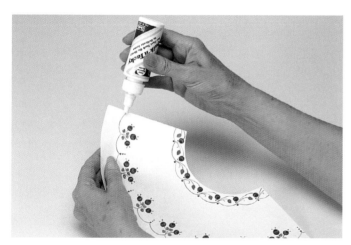

8 Varnish and Assemble Shade

Let dry. Remove pattern lines with a damp paper towel. Coat the shade with Delta Exterior/Interior Satin Varnish or Delta Stencil Magic Top Coat Satin Spray.

Let dry. Cut out the shade. Then apply glue to the painted side of the shade on the end that does not have diminishing dots. Curve the other end of the shade around and place it on top of the glue so the design lines up. You will have about ¼" (6mm) overlap.

Place a tea light in the flowerpot, light it and cover it with the shade.

Two Note Cards

Paper crafts are all the rage. This project shows how easy it is to add a painted border to paper for a personal touch.

Any paper craft technique can be used with borders, but I particularly like the effect of embossed stenciling. You'll find a large selection of these stencils in your hobby store. Add your special touch to a note card with an embossed center motif.

Corner motifs can add an extremely effective decorative touch. Even a simple design in the point of an envelope flap can make that envelope a keeper.

Materials

Surfaces
Hearts
- White note cards, 4½" × 5½" (11cm × 14cm)

Tulips
- Ivory note cards: 5" × 6½" (13cm × 17cm)

Paint *Delta Ceramcoat Acrylics*
Hearts

| Hydrangea Pink | Moss Green | Chambray Blue |

Tulips

| Moss Green | Wedgwood Green | Lilac |

| Lavender | Pale Lilac |

Loew-Cornell Brushes
Hearts
- No. 10/0 liner, series 7350C
- No. 2 round, series 7000
- No 2 filbert, series 7500

Tulips
- No. 10/0 liner, series 7350C
- No. 2 round, series 7000

Additional Supplies
Hearts
- Brass embossing stencil, hearts, #FS 804 (Judith Barker), from American Traditional Designs
- Tape
- Artograph Globox light box (or other light box)
- Double-end stylus or embossing tool
- Blue Super Chacopaper

Tulips
- Tracing paper and pencil
- Ruler
- Blue Super Chacopaper
- Stylus
- Paper towel
- Scissors

Specialized Supplies
A light box, double-end stylus and a brass embossing stencil are specialized but easy-to-find supplies used for the "Hearts" note card.

See page 137 for patterns.

Hearts Note Card

1 Position Stencil
Center the stencil on the face of the note card front and tape in place.

2 Emboss Stencil Design
Place the card on the light box surface with the stencil down. With a double-end stylus, trace around the edge of the stencil design, pressing hard enough to create the embossing. Use the larger ball for the larger openings and the smaller ball for the smaller areas.

3 Transfer Corner Pattern
Trace the pattern of the corner motif and then, using blue Chacopaper and a stylus, transfer it onto the four corners of the note card front and the lower left corner of the envelope. Make sure you transfer on the raised side of the embossed card.

4 Paint Hearts
Paint the raised hearts with Hydrangea Pink and a no. 2 filbert.

5 Paint Leaves and Stems
Paint the raised leaves and stems with Moss Green on a no. 2 round.

6 Paint Corner Linework
Paint the corner linework with Chambray Blue and a no. 10/0 liner. Let dry and then remove the tracing lines with a just barely damp paper towel.

Tulips Note Card

1 Trace and Transfer Patterns
Trace and transfer the note card and envelope patterns. Align the note card design so the bottom scallop is about ⅛"(3mm) from the bottom edge of the card front.

2 Base and Shade Leaves
Base the leaves with a Moss Green S-stroke applied with a no. 2 round. Then side load the brush in Wedgwood Green and, keeping the color to the outside, shade the leaves.

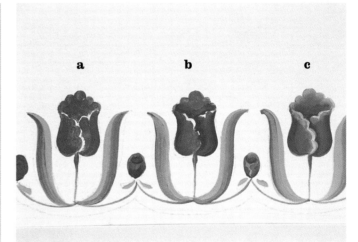

3 Paint Remaining Green Elements
For the rest of the greens, use the no. 10/0 liner. The strokes under the small flowers are Moss Green. The scalloped lines and stems are Wedgwood Green.

4 Paint Tulips
Both the large and the small tulips are painted with a no. 2 round:

a. Base with Lilac, being careful not to lose the "ruffles" between the petals.

b. Shade with side-loaded Lavender.

c. Highlight with side-loaded Pale Lilac.

5 Dot In Stamens, Cut Scalloped Edge

Dot in the stamens in the flower throats with Moss Green and a stylus. Let dry and carefully remove the Chacopaper lines with a just barely damp paper towel. Give the card a scalloped edge by cutting on the lower scalloped line.

Variation Tip

If you seldom or never send note cards, you can still decorate your envelopes. I frequently paint a floral design on my envelopes. Recipients tell me they love them!

Scrapbook *Page*

*f*or this project I designed a border for a 5" x 7" (13cm x 18cm) photo space. This border is simple enough that you can easily adjust the dimensions to fit your need. Of course, you could put other things inside the border besides a photo, as you see on the opposite page.

Actually, when designing for scrapbook pages, the positioning of photos and borders on the page may pose more of a challenge than the border dimensions. Getting two or three photos and their borders spaced just right on a page can take some advance planning. The basic principles for precise positioning are explained in the sidebar on page 54. The key is to create a tissue paper template and then make a few strategically placed folds.

On page 55 you'll find a couple of examples of attractive photo and border arrangements.

Materials

Surface

- Scrapbook page, 10" × 10" (25cm × 25cm)

Paint *Delta Paint for Paper*

Sunburst
Yellow

White

Sunburst
Yellow +
White (1:1)

Garden
Green

Loew-Cornell Brushes

- No. 10/0 liner, series 7350C
- No. 0 spotter, series 3650

Additional Supplies

- Tracing paper and pencil
- Ruler
- Blue Super Chacopaper
- Stylus

Specialized Supplies
Paint for paper and a spotter brush are specialized but easy-to-find supplies used for this project.

See page 137 for pattern.

Border *Positioning*

1 Trace and Transfer Pattern

Trace the pattern and transfer it onto a 10" x 10"(25cm x 25cm) scrapbook page with blue Chacopaper and a stylus. A ruler will help you keep the lines straight.

2 Paint Petals

Paint the flower petals with Sunburst Yellow + White (1:1) and a no. 0 spotter. Form each petal by pressing down the point of the brush and then lifting.

Positioning Elements on Scrapbook Pages

Use this procedure to determine the sizing and positioning of scrapbook photos and borders for different page layouts. Working out your border on tissue lets you experiment without soiling or marring your actual scrapbook page.

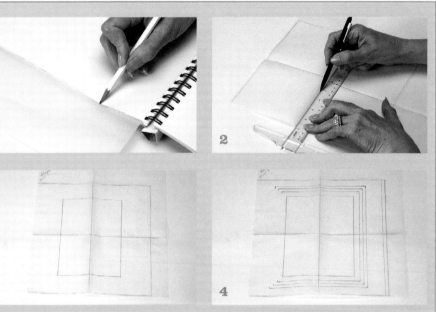

1 Create a Page Tracing

Create a tracing of your scrapbook page by placing tracing paper over the scrapbook page and rubbing the side of the pencil lead on the tracing paper over the edge of the scrapbook page.

2 Mark Photo Centerlines

Measure and mark off the centerlines for the area(s) where you want photo(s) to go. In this case, I want a space in the center of the page for a 5" x 7" (13cm x 18 cm) photo. To do this, first fold the tissue down the middle of the traced scrapbook page and mark the centerfold line with a pencil. Then fold the tissue tracing in half the other way and again mark the centerfold line.

Folding the tissue in thirds or fourths would enable you to place photos in other precise positions. If you prefer a more random scattering, simply arrange your photos on the tissue as you wish and draw outlines.

3 Mark Photo Space

Once you have your centerlines, you can measure and mark off the photo space. For a 5" x 7" (13cm x 18cm) vertically placed photo, your lines would be placed 2½" (6cm) from both sides of the vertical centerline and 3½" (9cm) from both sides of the horizontal centerline.

4 Draw Border Spine

Now draw in your border spine line(s) (see page 12), beginning at least ½" (13mm) from the line for the photo. Your particular border design will determine how many spines you need and how far apart they should be placed. Here you see three spines drawn ¼" (6mm) away from each other. From this point, continue to mark your section increments and helper dots as explained on page 12.

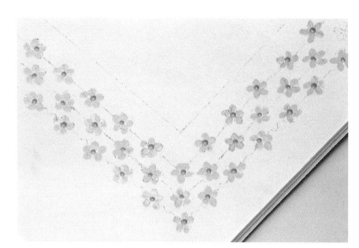

3 **Add Flower Centers**
Dot in the flower centers with Sunburst Yellow on a stylus. Reload the stylus for every dot so they'll stay uniform.

4 **Add Lifelines, Remove Transfer Lines**
Paint the lifelines between the flowers with Garden Green on a no. 10/0 liner. Let dry well. Using the spotter brush, dampen with water and remove any visible transfer lines. Don't get the scrapbook page too damp.

Gallery

Be creative! Scrapbook borders don't have to frame the photo space. They can separate photos or just decorate the page.

Wall *Border*

O ne problem with a long repeating border is that a tissue paper pattern will tend to wear out before you're through with it. To save yourself from frustration, trace your pattern on an acetate sheet, which will hold up to repeated transfers much longer.

A friend told me about the wall border paper used in this project, and I've had a lot of fun with it. I used this product to create the shade for the candle holder project (pages 42-45). In fact, you can use the flower pattern in this project to create a coordinating candle holder. This paper also comes in 27" (69cm) wide rolls, which can be used to create larger lamp shades.

Materials

Surface

- Wall-Liner for Borders, 6¹¹⁄₁₆" (17cm), no. ALLB6 from Eisenhart Wallcoverings Co., sold through Sherwin-Williams

Paint Delta Ceramcoat Acrylics

Periwinkle Blue   Blue Lagoon   Green Tea

Leprechaun   Chamomile

Stencil Magic Paint Creme

Cottage Blue

Loew-Cornell Brushes

- No. 18/0 liner, series 7350C
- ¼-inch (6mm) angular, series 7400

Additional Supplies

- Scissors
- Mini paint roller and pan
- Gesso
- Ruler or small T square
- Water erasable marking pen (available in fabric stores or departments)
- Acetate sheet and fine-point permanent marker
- Blue Super Chacopaper and ballpoint pen
- Stylus
- Delta Stencil Magic Pre-cut Decorative Stencil, Checkerboard Medley, #95-252-0012
- Masking tape
- Delta Repositional Stencil Adhesive Spray
- Paper towel
- ¼-inch (6mm) Delta Stencil Magic brush
- Wax paper
- Delta Stencil Magic Brush Cleaner
- Delta Stencil Magic Top Coat Satin Spray

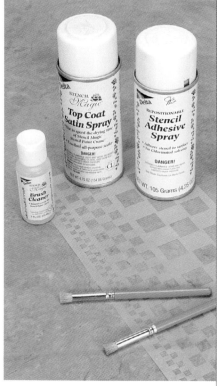

Specialized Supplies
A stencil, stencil brushes, Delta Stencil Magic Brush Cleaner, Delta Stencil MagicTop Coat Satin Spray and Delta stencil adhesive spray are specialized but easy-to-find supplies used for this project.

See page 138 for pattern.

Long Repeating Border

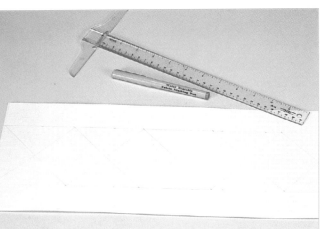

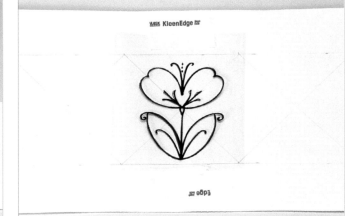

1 Base, Mark Off Sections

Cut an appropriate length of Wall-Liner for your wall. Using a mini paint roller, base the Wall-Liner with gesso on the side you will paint the border and allow it to dry well.

Measure in 1½"(4cm) from the upper and lower border edges and draw lines with a water erasable marking pen. Measure off 3½" (9cm) sections on these lines. Use these markings to draw diagonals between the top and bottom border lines to determine the center of each section.

2 Trace and Align Pattern

Trace the pattern onto an acetate sheet with a permanent marker. Line up the pattern so the petal indentations fall on the diagonals and the top of the stem falls on the intersection of the diagonals.

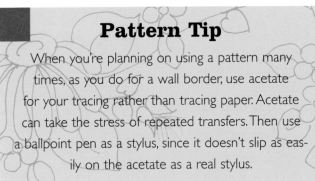

Pattern Tip

When you're planning on using a pattern many times, as you do for a wall border, use acetate for your tracing rather than tracing paper. Acetate can take the stress of repeated transfers. Then use a ballpoint pen as a stylus, since it doesn't slip as easily on the acetate as a real stylus.

3 Transfer design

Transfer the design with blue Chacopaper and a ballpoint pen. Do not transfer the strokes inside the petals and leaves at this time.

4 Base and Shade Petals and Leaves

Base the petals with two coats of Periwinkle Blue, using a ¼-inch (6mm) angular. Shade with side-loaded Blue Lagoon from the stem to the indentation. Base the leaves with Green Tea and a ¼-inch (6mm) angular. Shade the bottoms with side-loaded Leprechaun.

5 Highlight Leaves, Paint Stems, Strokes, Dots

Now transfer the petal and leaf strokes. Highlight the leaf tops with a side load of Chamomile on a ¼-inch (6mm) angular. Then use a no. 18/0 liner loaded with Chamomile to pull a line from the bottom of the stem up the top of the leaf and around the curl. With the same brush, paint the stem and the hook strokes in the leaves with Leprechaun. Use Green Tea for the hook strokes between the petals. The strokes on the petals are done with the no. 18/0 liner and Chamomile. Apply the diminishing dots (see page 11) with Chamomile and a stylus.

6 Stencil Top Checks

Mask off the large and small checks. Spray one side of the stencil with stencil adhesive so it will stick to the Wall-Liner while you're painting. Let dry 10 or 15 minutes. Line up the bottoms of the medium checks on the top drawn border line. Remove Chacopaper tracing lines in the stencil area with a damp paper towel. Apply Cottage Blue Stencil Magic Paint Creme with a ¼-inch (6mm) stencil brush. Continue repositioning the stencil until you finish the top checks. (The stencil can be moved several times before respraying with adhesive.)

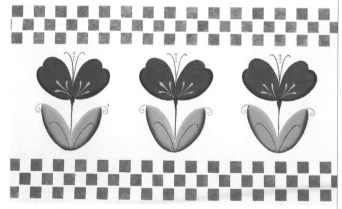

7 Stencil Bottom Checks

When you stencil the bottom checks, be sure you line up the squares with those you already stenciled on the top. Align the stencil on the drawn border line as you did for the top. When you're finished with the stencil, lay it on wax paper and clean it with Delta Stencil Magic Brush Cleaner.

Let the border dry. Remove remaining Chacopaper lines with a damp paper towel. Spray with Delta Stencil Magic Top Coat Satin Spray.

Completed Border

Elizabeth's *Trunk*

i designed this trunk for my granddaughter. Maybe you have a special person for whom you could paint this piece. Whether you give it away or keep it, don't forget to sign and date your work. Someday it could appear on the *Antiques Roadshow!*

Look closely at this design and you'll realize it's almost entirely composed of borders and embellishments, proving that border-based designs are appropriate for large as well as small objects. What's more, although the design looks complicated, there's actually little more to it than a few easy-to-paint flowers and some linework. Don't be afraid to try this project. Just take it step by step.

Materials

Surfaces

- 23" × 12½" × 14" (58cm × 32cm × 36cm) wooden trunk, Stan Brown Arts & Crafts # 97-01310

Paint *Delta Ceramcoat Acrylics*

Light Ivory   Candlelight   Seminole Green

Pine Green   Peony   Roman Stucco

Fruit Punch   Burnt Sienna   White

Blue Bayou   Passion

Loew-Cornell Brushes

- No. 18/0 script liner, series 7050
- No 2 round, series 7000
- No. 5 round, series 7000
- ¼-inch (6mm) angular, series 7400
- No. 4 filbert, series 7500
- No. 8 filbert, series 7500
- 1-inch (25mm) wash, series 7550, or disposable foam brushes for sealing, basing and varnishing (See "Brushes," page 6.)

Additional Supplies

- Tracing paper and pencil
- Delta All-Purpose Sealer
- Sanding pad
- Tack cloth or damp paper towel
- Mini paint roller and pan
- T square
- Chalk pencil
- Painter's Tape or other masking tape
- Blue Super Chacopaper
- Stylus
- Cotton swabs
- Delta Exterior/Interior Satin Varnish

See page 138-141 for patterns.

Borders *on Large Object*

1 Prepare the Surface

Trace the design onto tracing paper and set aside. Seal the trunk with All-Purpose Sealer. Let dry and then sand. Remove the sanding dust with a tack cloth or damp paper towel. Use a mini paint roller to apply two basecoats of Light Ivory to the entire trunk, sanding lightly between coats. Using a T square and chalk pencil, measure and mark off the 2" (5cm) outside bands on the trunk front, top and sides. Place masking tape along these marks and basecoat the bands with Candlelight, using a 1-inch (25mm) wash brush or disposable foam brush. Note that the trunk back is entirely Light Ivory and has no bands. Let the paint dry well. Remove the tape. Sand lightly to remove any ridges between the two base colors. Transfer the patterns.

Highlighting Daisy Petals

Use this technique when highlighting the daisy petals in step 4c.

1 Load the Brush

When you highlight the daisy petals, you will also be building texture with a thick paint layer. This is accomplished by loading a no. 5 round in Peony and then scooping a "fingertip" of White on the tip.

2 Stroke the Petal

Stroke from the outer tip of the petal toward the base. The heavy brush load will leave a raised layer of white in some places. The border daisy petals are highlighted the same way, but with a no. 2 round stroke.

2 Base, Shade and Highlight Large Leaves

Base the large leaves with two coats of Seminole Green on a no. 8 filbert, painting carefully around the daisy petals. Using the same brush, side load and shade with Pine Green under the petals, where the leaves overlap and along the leaf centers. Still with the same brush, reload in Seminole Green and wipe off excess paint on a paper towel. Then side load in Candlelight and highlight beside the leaf-center shading and along some outside edges.

3 Paint Violet, Bellflower and Border Daisy Leaves

Using a no. 5 round, base the violet and bellflower leaves in Pine Green. Note that the bellflower leaves are heart-shaped but the violet leaves have a flat base. To highlight the leaf centers, reload the brush in Pine Green, wipe off the excess paint and side load in Seminole Green. Paint the daisy leaves in the border using the same colors and technique as you did with the large leaves in step 2. Use the no. 5 round.

4 Paint the Daisies

a. Base the Daisy petals with Peony. Use a no. 5 round on the large daisies in the middle panels and a no. 2 round for the small border daisies. Base the daisy centers with Roman Stucco, again using the no. 5 round on the large and the no. 2 round on the small.

b. Using Fruit Punch on a no. 18/0 script liner, pull fine "gathering stroke" lines from the base of the petals out, following the petal curves. Then use a no. 5 round to overpaint the petals with a wash of Peony, softening the Fruit Punch lines.

Side load a no. 4 filbert with Burnt Sienna and tap in shading on the outer edge of all the daisy centers. On the large daisies only, also tap in a "C" shape inside the flower center, creating a "button."

c. Highlight the daisy centers with White on a no. 4 filbert. For the

larger daisies, place this on the top of the button centers and around the button in an offset oval. For the smaller daisies, highlight opposite the shading.

At this point you will highlight the daisy petals. See the sidebar on the opposite page for instructions.

Finish the daisies by side loading the toe of a ¼-inch (6mm) angular with thin Fruit Punch and tapping in a feathery stroke at the base of each petal. Make this darker on the back petals than on the front. Use less pressure on the border flowers to accommodate the smaller petals.

5 Paint the Violets

Paint the violet petals with Passion side-loaded on a no. 4 filbert, keeping the color to the outside. Dot in the flower centers with Roman Stucco on a stylus.

6 Paint the Bellflowers

Paint the bellflowers in two strokes with a no. 2 round and Blue Bayou. Add stamens with a no. 18/0 script liner and Seminole Green. Use Roman Stucco on a stylus to dot in pollen.

Borders *on Large Object*

7 Pull Stems and Tendrils

Pull all the stems and tendrils with a no. 18/0 script liner. Make the stems Pine Green and the tendrils Seminole Green.

8 Dab in Background Color

Use a no. 5 round loaded with extremely thin Seminole Green to dab in background color behind the daisies. Immediately blend by patting with your fingertip. If the paint gets on the petals, remove it with a damp cotton swab or restroke the petal.

9 Paint Shadow Leaves and Border Line

Randomly fill space around the large daisies and stems with one-stroke shadow leaves. Use very thin Seminole Green on a no. 5 round. Then with slightly thinned Seminole Green, paint the line border around the panel with a no. 18/0 script liner. There is no line at the top of the front and side panels.

10 Paint Lid Border and Varnish

Except for the dots, the lid border is painted with a no. 18/0 script liner. Use Blue Bayou for the scallops, applying more pressure in the middle to make the stroke wider. Use Seminole Green for the paired hook strokes, Peony for the stroke in the "V" of the paired hook strokes and Passion for the dashes. Paint the dots with White on a stylus. Let dry. Remove visible transfer lines and then varnish.

Front

Top

Side

Three-Step **Borders**

Dogwood

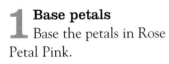

1 **Base petals**
Base the petals in Rose Petal Pink.

2 **Shade Petals**
Shade the petals in Sweetheart Blush.

3 **Paint Centers and Details**
Paint the flower centers in Brown Velvet. Use the same color to edge the petals. Dot the center with Moss Green.

Lilacs and Daisies

1 **Stipple in Lilacs**
Stipple the lilacs with Lilac. Repeat with Deep Lilac.

2 **Paint Daisies**
Paint the daisies White with Light Timberline Green center dots.

3 **Paint Leaves**
Add Dark Foliage Green leaves to the lilacs. Paint the daisy leaves in a brush-mix of Light Foliage Green + Medium Foliage Green.

Lavender Daisies

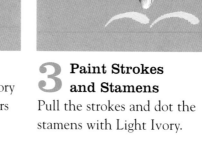

1 **Paint Leaves**
Base the leaves in Eucalyptus and highlight in Sea Grass.

2 **Paint Daisies**
Paint the petals in Light Ivory + Eggplant. Paint the daisy centers in Dark Goldenrod.

3 **Paint Strokes and Stamens**
Pull the strokes and dot the stamens with Light Ivory.

Poppies

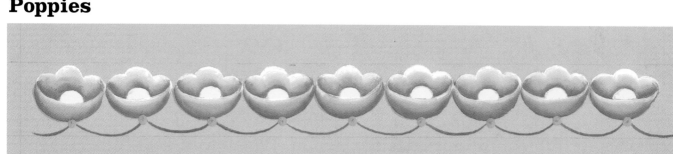

1 **Base Poppies**
Base the back petals in Western Sunset Yellow, the front petals in Island Coral and the poppy centers in Pale Yellow

2 **Shade and Highlight Petals**
Shade the petals in Coral. Highlight with White.

3 **Add Linework and Dots**
Paint Coral connecting lines. Dot Island Coral at the base of the poppies.

Three-Step Borders

Tole Tulips

1 Base and Shade Tulip
Base the tulips in Wild Rose. Shade in Maroon.

2 Highlight and Connect
Highlight the tulips in Light Ivory. Use the same color and a liner to paint the connecting lines.

3 Add Strokes and Stamens
Paint Light Ivory strokes with a Maroon dot at their base. Paint Maroon stamens and Light Ivory stamen dots.

Peach Flowers

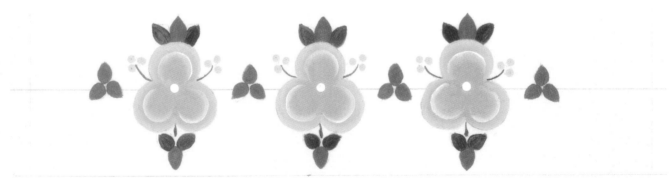

1 Paint Leaves and Flowers
Paint all leaves except side leaves above and below flowers in Green Sea. Stems and remaining leaves are Medium Foliage Green. Base flowers in Island Coral.

2 Highlight Petals
Highlight the petal edges in Santa's Flesh. Add a White inner highlight.

3 Add Dots
Paint the three-dot flowers in Santa's Flesh. Dot the center of the main flowers with White.

Red Flowers

1 Paint Petals
Base the petals in Tuscan Red. Add Maroon gathering lines.

2 Paint Linework
Paint the linework White.

3 Add Strokes and Dots
Paint strokes and small side dots Medium Foliage Green. Paint the flower centers and large side dots Empire Gold. Add White center dots to the flowers.

Roses

1 Base the Roses
Base the ball of the roses in Nectar Coral and the outer petals in Hydrangea Pink.

2 Shade and Highlight
Shade the roses with Deep Coral. Highlight with White.

3 Paint Strokes, Dots and Lines
Add White strokes and dots. Paint the connecting lines in Medium Foliage Green.

Three-Step Borders

Pink Tulips

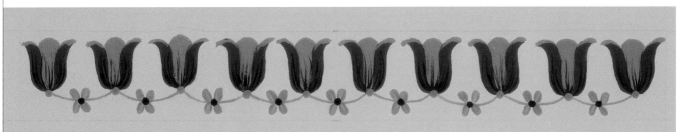

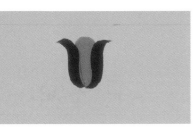

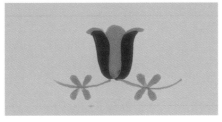

1 Base Tulips
Base the tulip centers in Pink Quartz. Use an S-stroke to paint Raspberry outer petals.

2 Finish Petals and Add Stems
Stroke on top of the outer petals in Pink Quartz. Paint the small flowers in the same color. Add Light Foliage Green stem lines.

3 Paint Gathering Lines and Dots
Add Barn Red gathering lines to the tulips. Dot centers in the small flowers with the same color. Add a Pink Quartz dot at the tulip bases.

Four-square Tulips

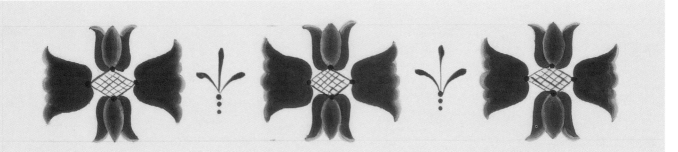

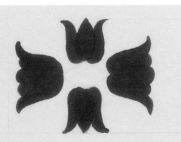

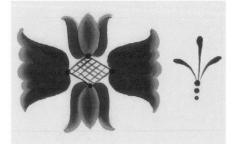

1 Base Tulips
Base the small tulips' outside petals in Poppy Orange. Base the large tulips and small tulips' center petals in Rouge.

2 Shade and Highlight
Shade the large tulips in Poppy Orange and highlight all tulips in Hydrangea Pink.

3 Add Crosshatching, Dots and Strokes
Paint crosshatching, dots and strokes Medium Foliage Green. Add Poppy Orange diminishing dots.

Orange and Yellow Daisies

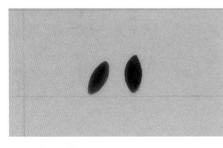

1 Base Leaves
Base the leaves in Deep River Green.

2 Paint Petals
Brush mix Tuscan Red + Crocus Yellow to paint the petals.

3 Add Finishing Details
Paint the center dots, stems, hook strokes and leaf vein strokes in Medium Foliage Green.

"Ball" Flowers

1 Base Leaves and Stems
Base leaves and stems in Pine Green.

2 Base Flowers
Base the balls and petals in Opaque Red.

3 Add Shading and Strokes
Shade the balls in Barn Red. Add Light Foliage Green leaf strokes.

Three-Step Borders

Strokes and Linework 1

1 Start with Linework
Paint the wavy linework in Bungalow Blue.

2 Add Blue Strokes
Paint the large strokes in Coastline Blue.

3 Paint Hooks and Dots
Paint the hook strokes and dots in White.

Strokes and Linework 2

1 Paint Triangles and Large Strokes
Paint the top triangles and large strokes in Medium Foliage Green. Paint the bottom triangles in Dark Foliage Green.

2 Add Green Detailing
Paint curly strokes and dot triangle tips with Sea Grass.

3 Add Gold Detailing
Add Metallic 14K Gold small strokes and descending dots.

Strokes and Linework 3

1 Start with Scrolls
Paint scrolls in Mediterranean.

2 Add Large Strokes
Paint the large strokes in Wild Rose.

3 Embellish with Strokes, Lines and Dots
Paint small strokes, connecting lines and dots in Paradise.

Strokes and Linework 4

1 Paint Curly Linework
Paint the curly bracket linework in Green Sea.

2 Start Strokes and Finish Lines
Paint the largest strokes, connecting lines and linework strokes in Old Parchment.

3 Finish Strokes and Add Dots
Paint Moss Green strokes on both sides of the Old Parchment strokes. Paint remaining strokes and connecting line dots in Green Sea. The center dots are Old Parchment.

Three-Step Borders

Coffee Pot

1 Base and Shade Pots and Cups
Base the pots and cups in Navy Blue. Shade in Blue Velvet. Add Glacier Blue steam lines.

2 Stipple
Stipple pots and cups with White.

3 Add Details
Paint the lid knobs, lids, cup rims and top of spouts White.

Plates and Cups

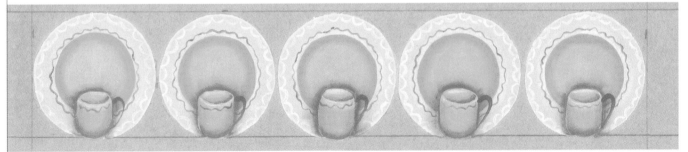

1 Base Plates and Cups
Base the plate rims in Rose Petal Pink, the plate centers in Rose Petal Pink + thinned Hydrangea Pink, and the cups in Rose Petal Pink + Hydrangea Pink.

2 Shade, Highlight and Add Handles
Shade the cups and plate centers in Hydrangea Pink. Highlight the cup rims with White. Paint Pink Quartz cup handles.

3 Add Finishing Details
Shade behind the cups with White. Add White scalloped trim on the outer plate edges. Add Pink Quartz trim around the plate centers and on cup rims.

Cookies and Milk

1 Base Cookie Jars, Paint Glasses and Milk
Base the cookie jars in Stonewedge Green. Paint the glasses with side-loaded Soft Grey. Paint in White milk.

2 Shade and Highlight
Shade the jars with Deep River Green. Tap a White highlight in the centers of the jars. Also highlight the lids and the glasses.

3 Add Lettering and Details
Paint the lettering, lid knobs and jar bases in Deep River Green.

Apple Pies

1 Base Pies and Apples
Base the pies in Mocha Brown and the apples in Medium Foliage Green.

2 Shade and Add Pie Details
Shade the pies and add crust details with Brown Velvet. Shade the apples with Dark Foliage Green.

3 Highlight Apples, Add Stems and Leaves
Highlight the apples in Sea Grass. Add Brown Velvet stems and Medium Foliage Green leaves.

Three-Step Borders

Grapes

1 Base Grapes
Fill in the grapes with Eggplant.

2 Shade and Highlight Grapes
Shade the grapes with Purple. Highlight with Passion.

3 Paint Leaves and Add Lines
Base the leaves in Timberline Green. Shade with Avocado and highlight with White. Add Avocado connecting lines.

Sun

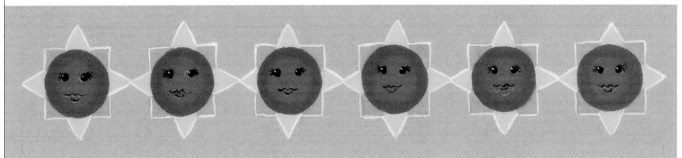

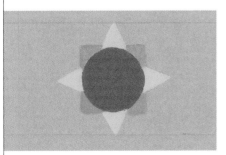  

1 Base
Base the round part of the suns in Dark Goldenrod, the long rays in Crocus Yellow and the short rays in Straw.

2 Outline Rays and Shade Suns
Outline the rays in Pale Yellow. Shade the round suns in Pumpkin.

3 Paint Faces
Paint Navy Blue eyes with Burnt Sienna lashes. Highlight the eyes with White dots. Add Rouge mouths.

Cozy Cottage

1 **Base Houses and Trunks**
Base the houses in Blue Wisp, the windows in Crocus Yellow and the doors in Autumn Brown. Base the trees in Brown Velvet.

2 **Add House Details**
Continuing with Brown Velvet, paint the roofs, outline the doors and windowpanes and dot in the doorknobs. Shade under the roofs with Blue Haze.

3 **Paint Leaves, Flowers and Door Crowns**
Stipple treetops in Medium Foliage Green, then Dark Foliage Green. Dot Pink Quartz flowers with White highlights. Add Medium Foliage Green stems and leaves. Paint White door crowns.

Umbrellas

1 **Base Umbrella Tops**
Base the umbrella tops in Medium Victorian Teal.

2 **Shade and Highlight Umbrella Tops**
Shade the umbrella tops in Dark Victorian Teal and highlight in Light Victorian Teal.

3 **Finish Umbrellas and Add Raindrops**
Paint the handles, rib tips and top buttons with Brown Velvet. Add Blue Velvet raindrops.

Three-Step Borders

Straw Hats

1 **Base Hats and Bands**
Base the straw hats in Spice Tan and the hatbands in Blue Wisp.

2 **Add Lines, Shading and Highlighting**
Paint Light Ivory weaving lines. Shade the hats in Burnt Sienna. Highlight the bands in White.

3 **Paint Roses and Leaves**
Paint the roses in swirls of Tuscan Red and White. Add Medium Foliage Green leaves.

Roosters

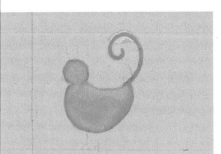  

1 **Base Roosters**
Base the rooster heads and bodies in Empire Gold. Use the same color for the longest tail feathers.

2 **Shade and Highlight**
Shade with Burnt Sienna. Highlight with Pale Yellow.

3 **Add Finishing Details**
Paint eyes, beaks, wings, feet and short tail feathers with Burnt Sienna. Paint medium tail feathers, wing strokes and head curls with Pale Yellow. Line beneath the head curls with Empire Gold.

Sweethearts

1 Outline the Large Hearts
Outline the large hearts with Opaque Red.

2 Paint Lips and Small Hearts
Paint the lips and small hearts with Opaque Red.

3 Paint the Faces
Paint the cheeks with side-loaded Opaque Red. Paint noses and lip corners with Opaque Red. Paint the eyes White with Black pupils, outlines and lashes. Add a White highlight to the pupils.

Bunnies

1 Base Bunnies
Base the bunnies in White.

2 Shade Bunnies and Add Tails
Shade the bunnies in Bridgeport Grey. Add White tail dots.

3 Paint Grass
Using Light, Medium and Dark Foliage Green, paint a baseline for the grass and then pull blades.

Three-Step Borders

Jack-o'-lanterns and Ghosts

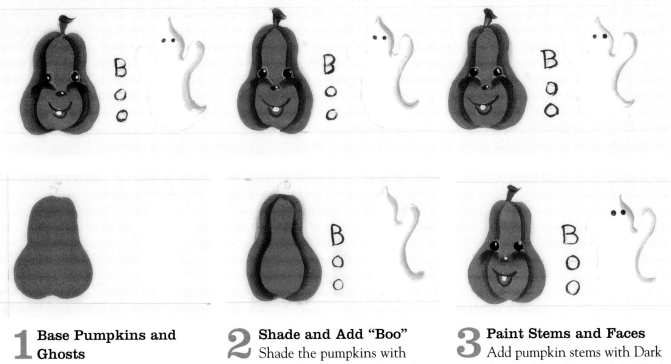

1 Base Pumpkins and Ghosts
Base the pumpkins in Pumpkin and the ghosts in White.

2 Shade and Add "Boo"
Shade the pumpkins with Orange and the ghosts with Quaker Grey. Add the word, *Boo*, in Black.

3 Paint Stems and Faces
Add pumpkin stems with Dark + Medium Foliage Green. Add Black ghost and pumpkin eyes. Add Orange pumpkin mouths and noses. Side load Orange for cheeks. Add White eyes, nose highlights and teeth.

Candles

1 Base and Shade Candles
Base candles in Tuscan Red and shade in Barn Red.

2 Paint Leaves
Paint Dark Foliage Green leaves.

3 Paint Flames and Holders
Add Straw candle flames and Metallic Copper candle holders.

Teddy Bear Soldiers

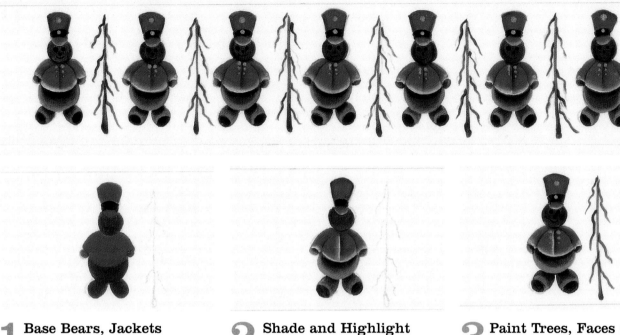

1 Base Bears, Jackets and Hats

Base the bears in Autumn Brown, the jackets and hats in Blue Lagoon and the hatbands in Crimson.

2 Shade and Highlight Bears, Jackets and Hats

Shade the bears in Brown Velvet and highlight in Light Chocolate. Shade the jackets and hats in Navy Blue and highlight in White.

3 Paint Trees, Faces and Gold Details

Paint Brown Velvet tree trunks and Deep River Green branches. Add Black face features and Metallic 14K Gold buttons and hat embellishments.

Bells and Ribbons

1 Base Bells and Ribbons

Base the bells with Truly Teal and the ribbon garlands with Deep Coral.

2 Shade and Highlight Ribbons

Shade the ribbon garlands with Sweetheart Blush and then highlight with White.

3 Paint Details

Add ribbon knots with a swirl of Deep Coral and White. Add Sweetheart Blush bell ties and clappers. Paint a White band at the bottom of the bells.

Hundreds of Borders

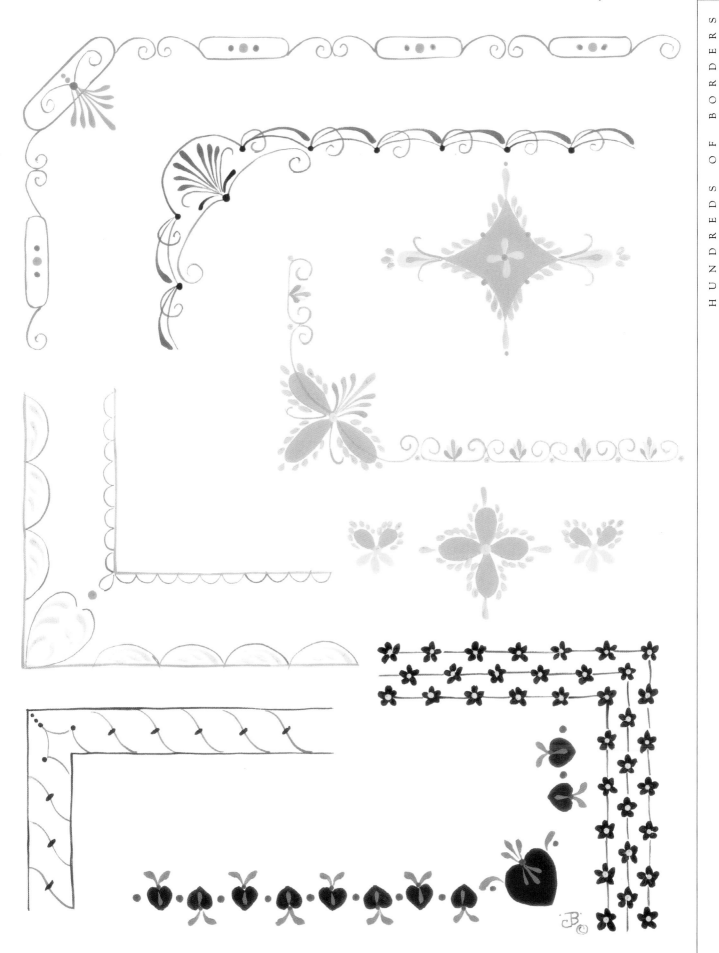

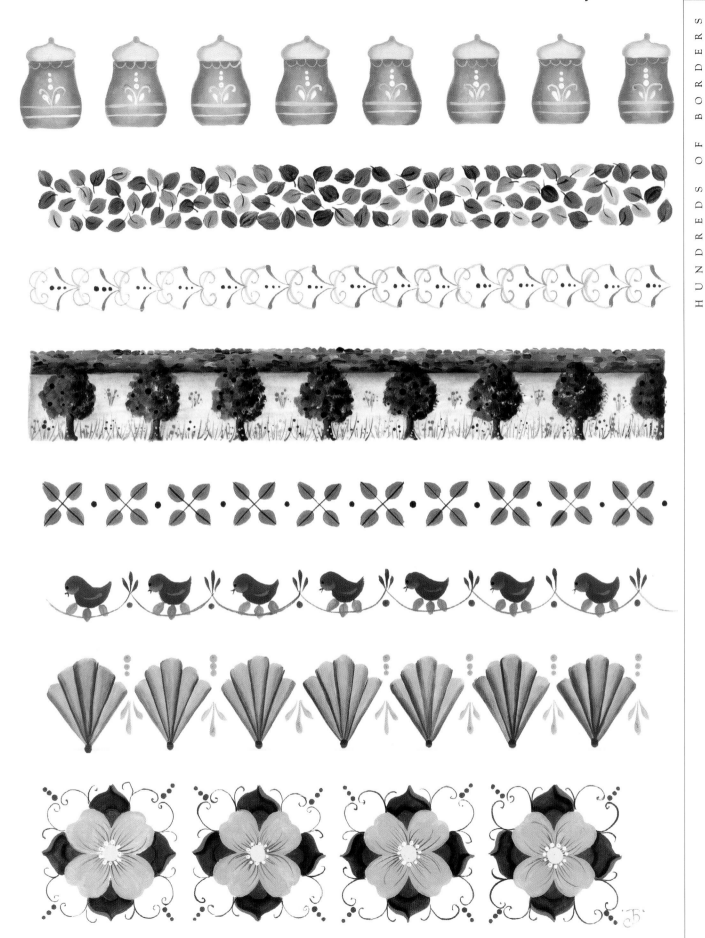

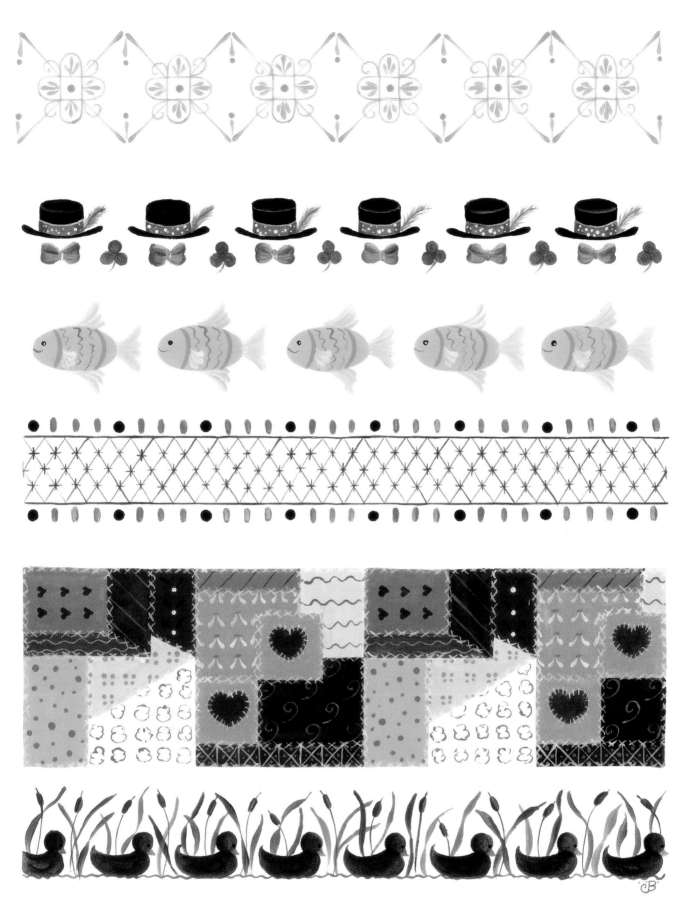

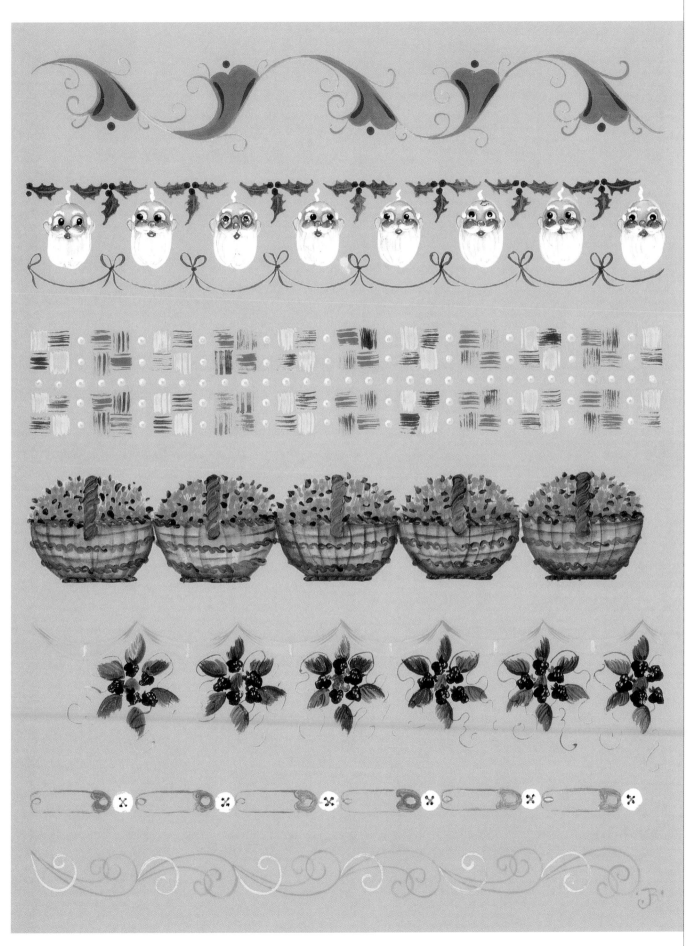

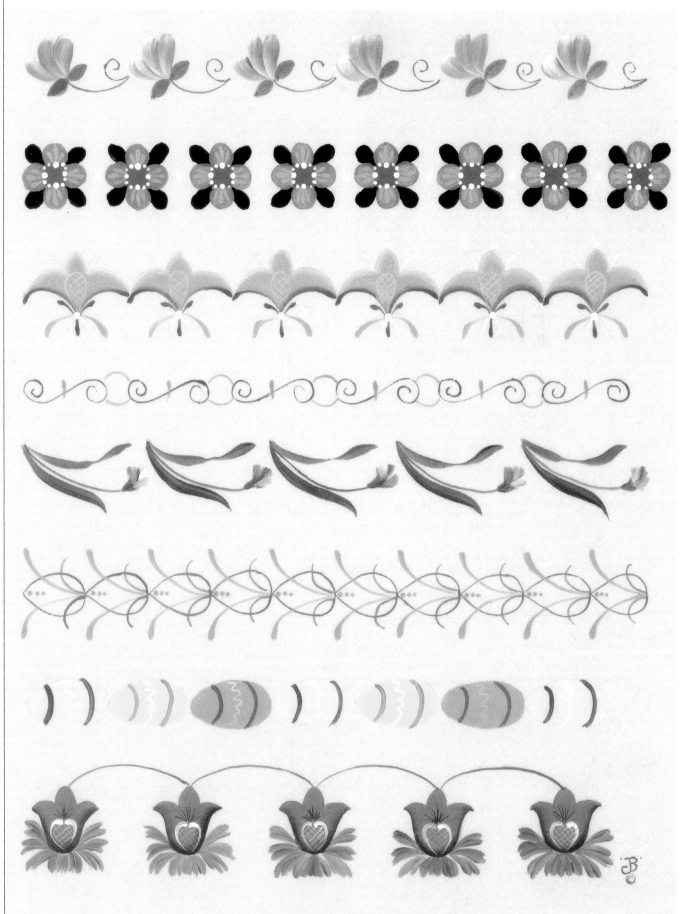

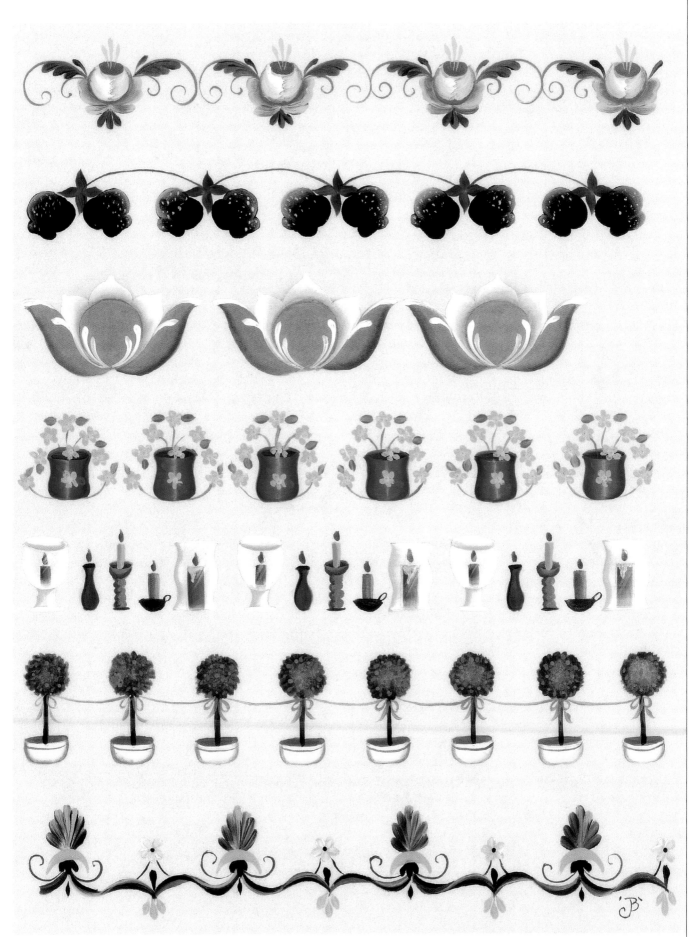

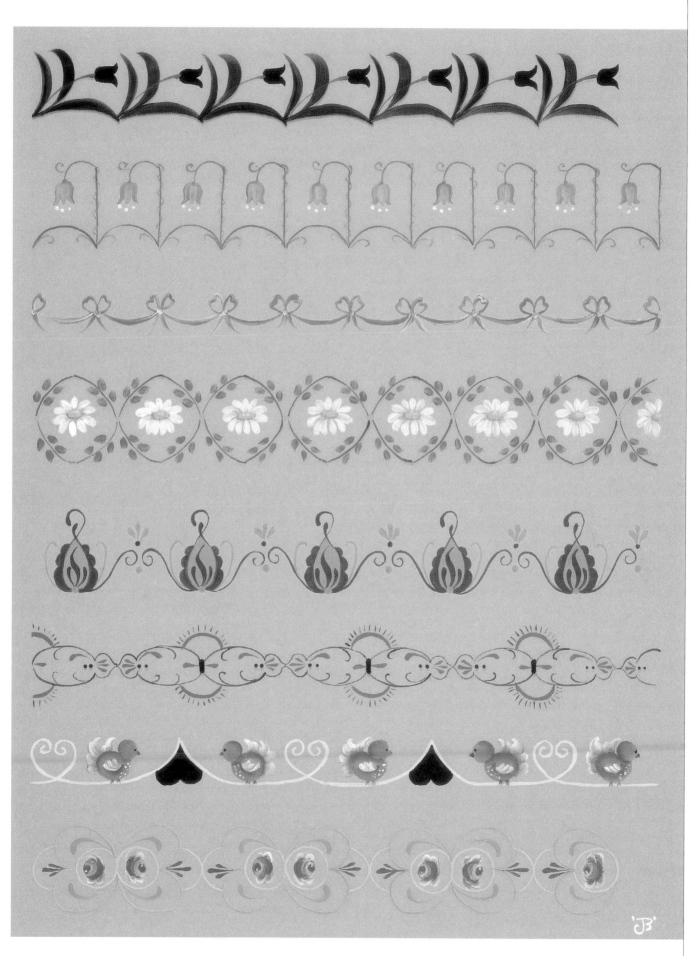

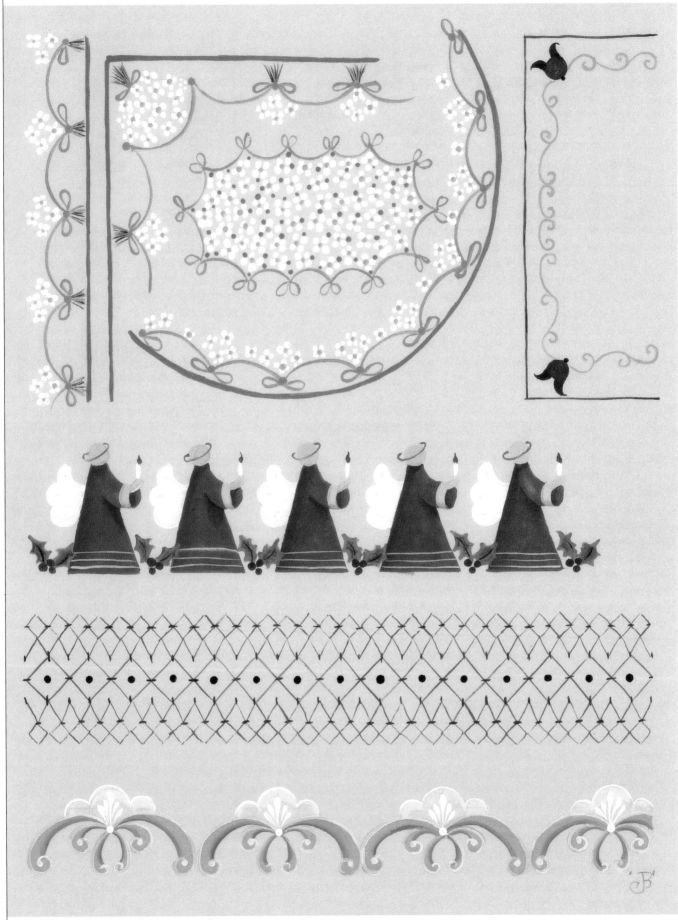

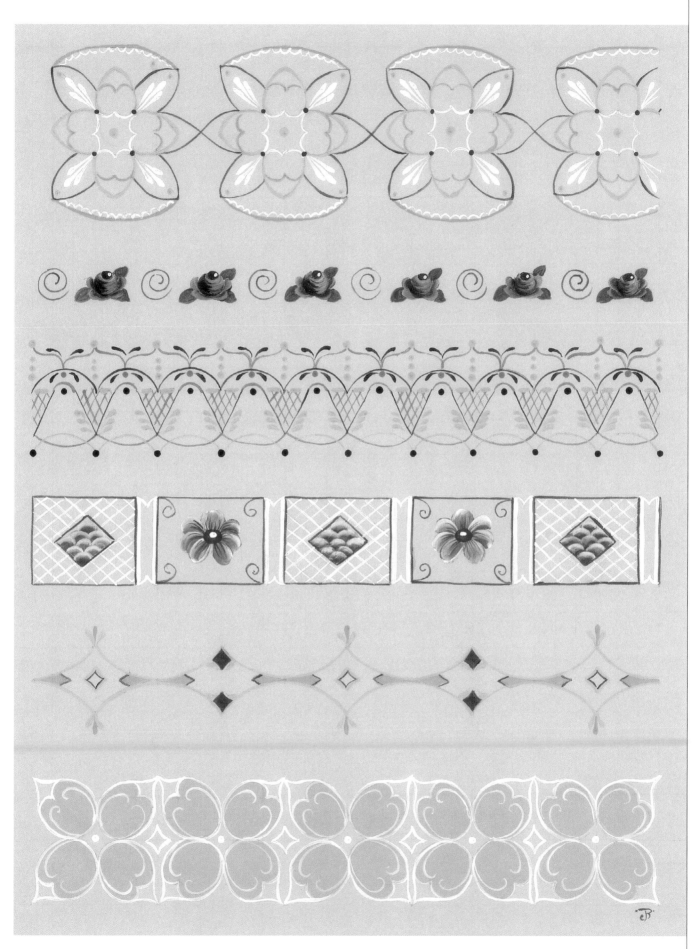

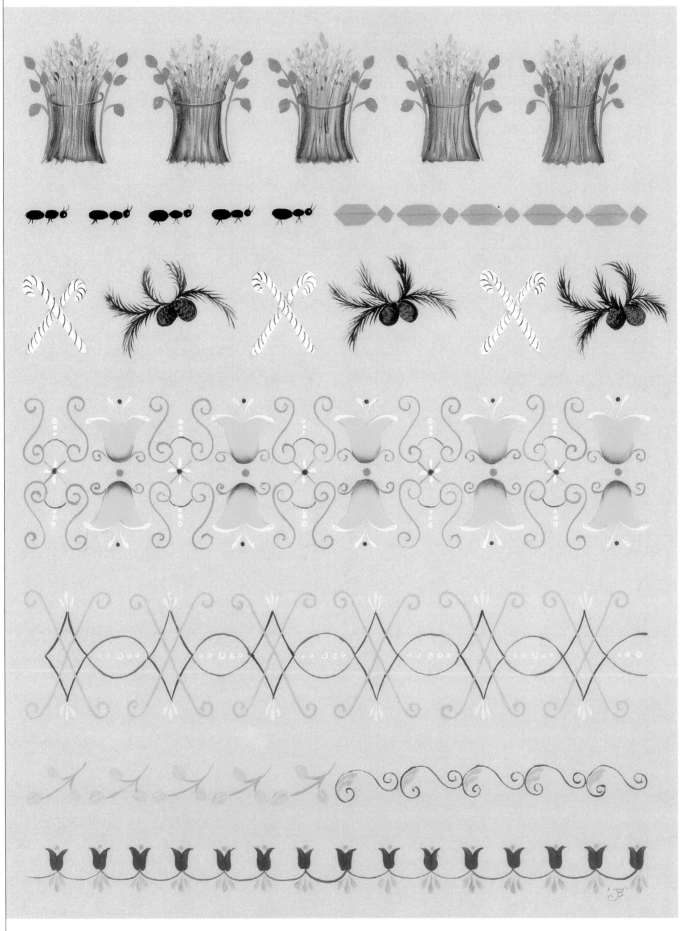

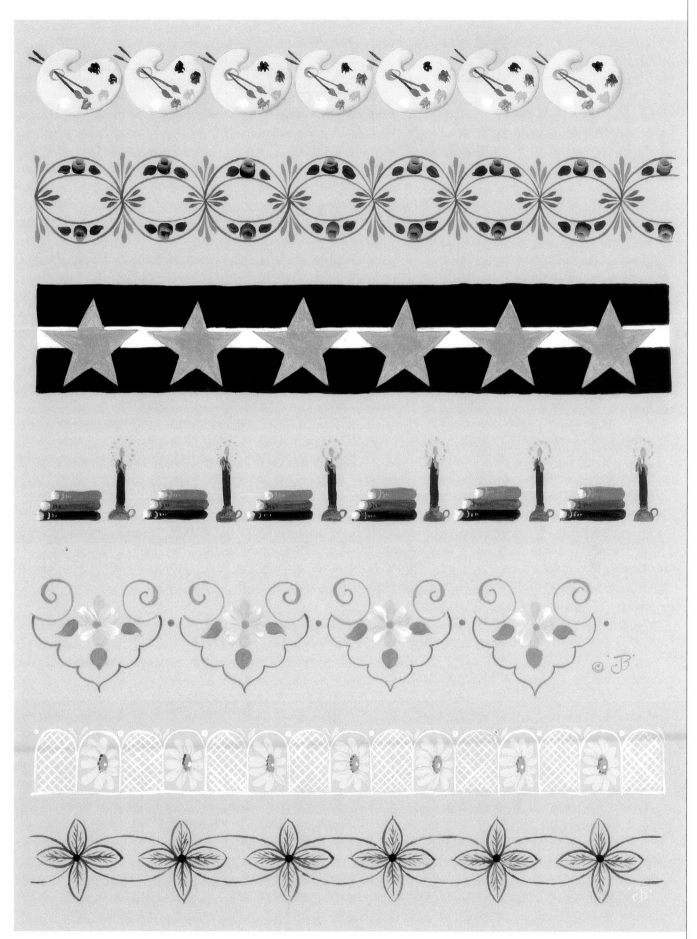

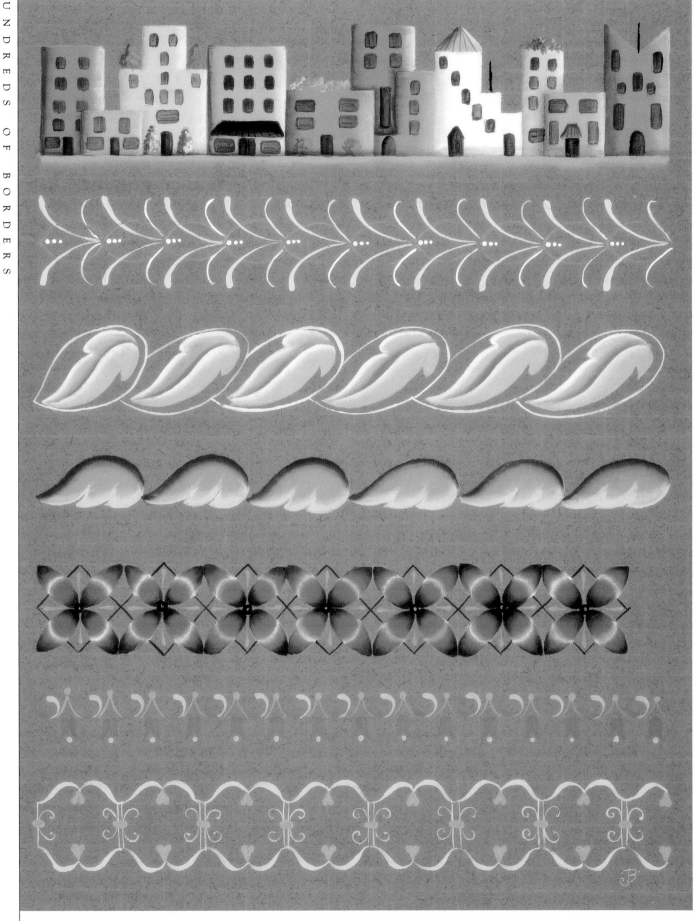

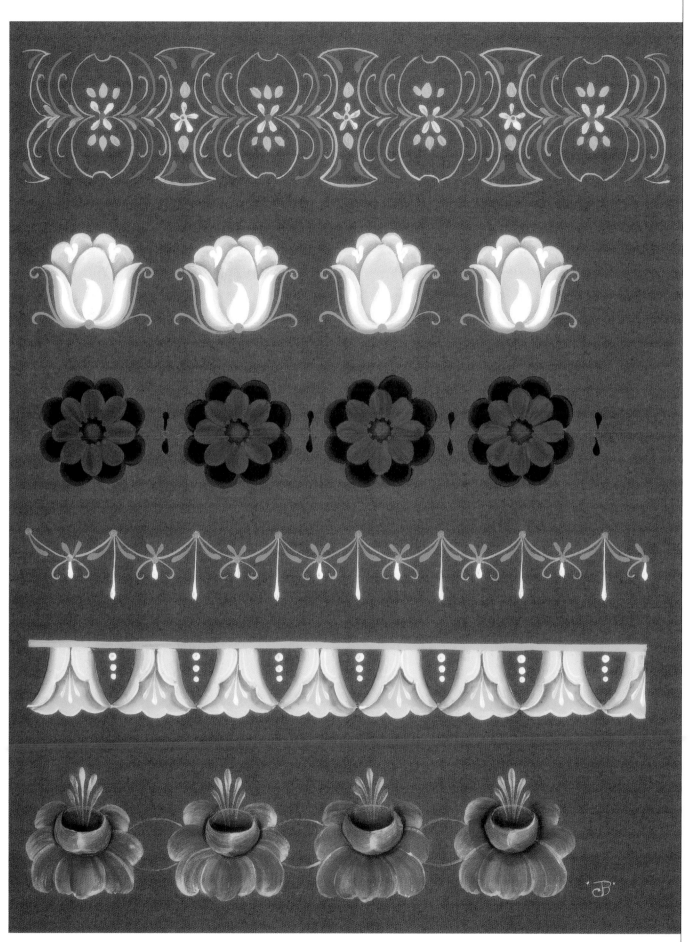

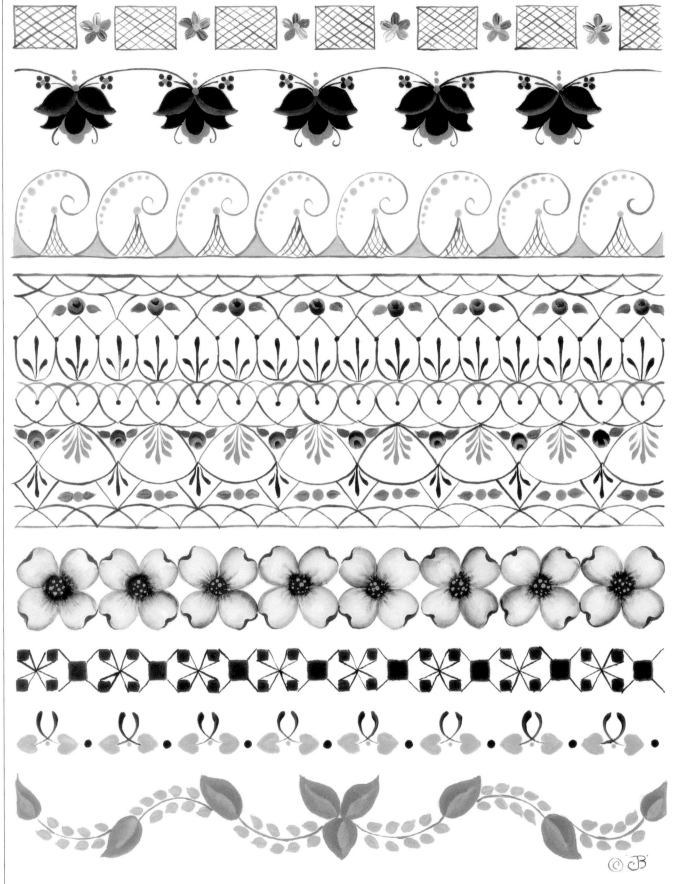

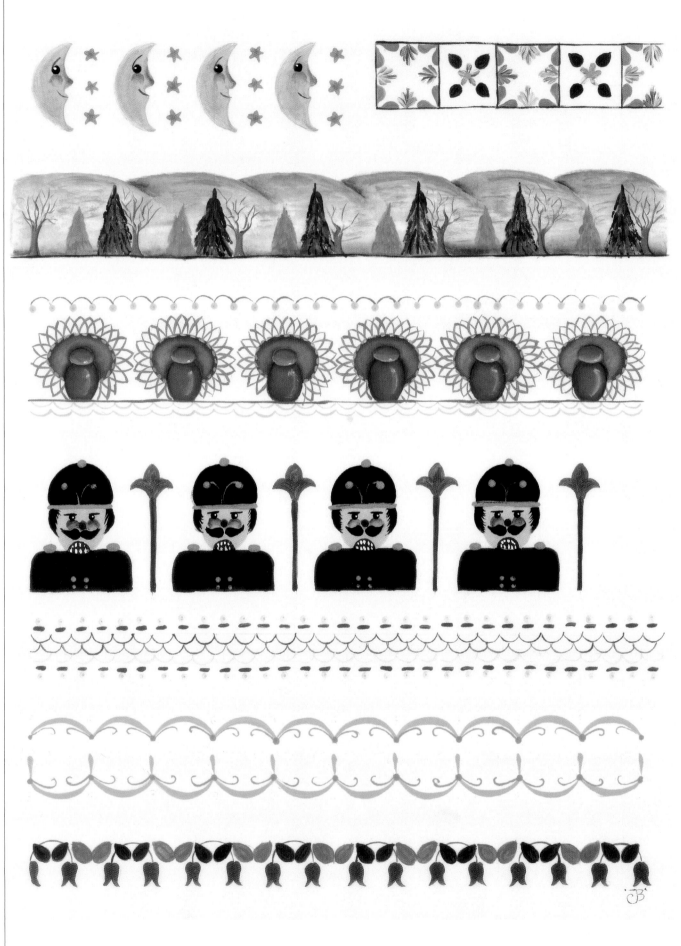

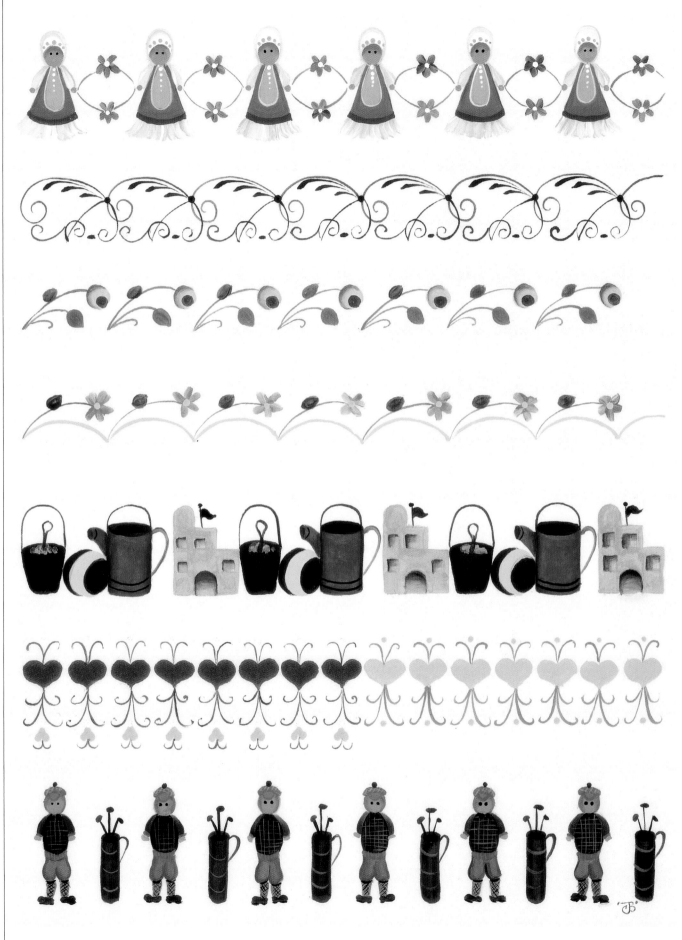

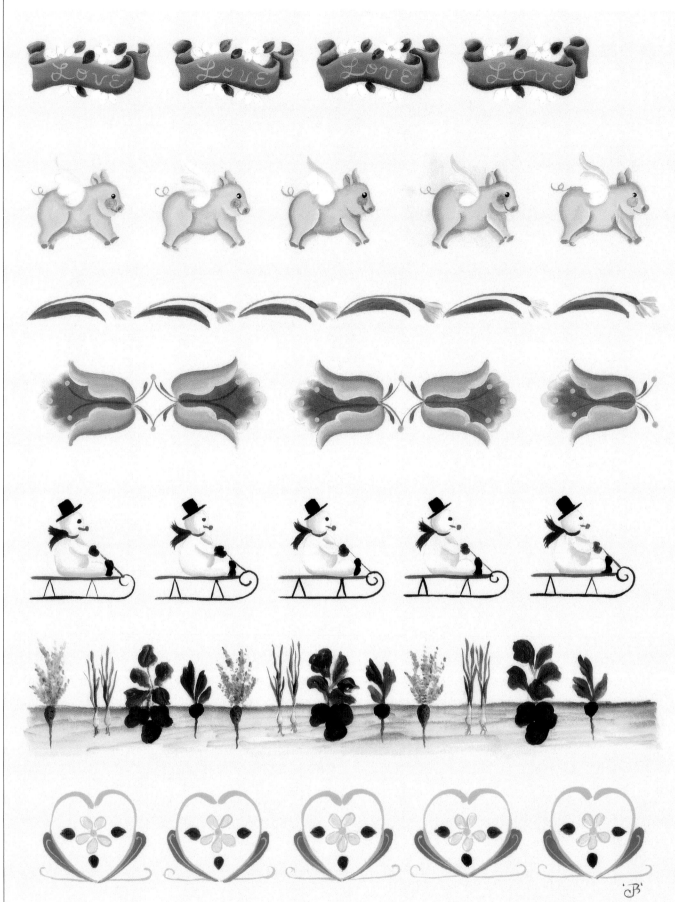

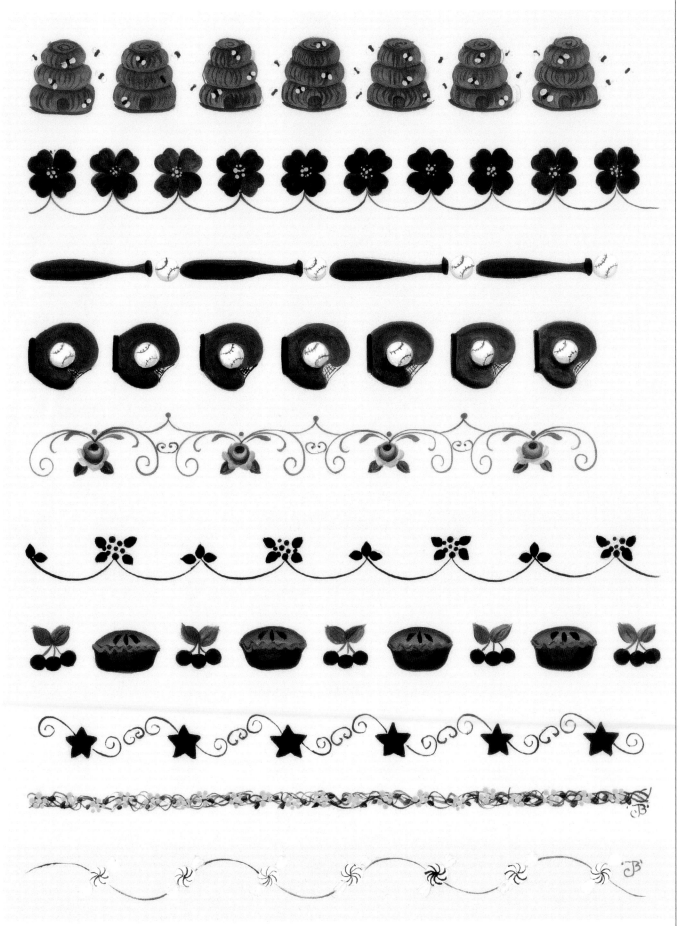

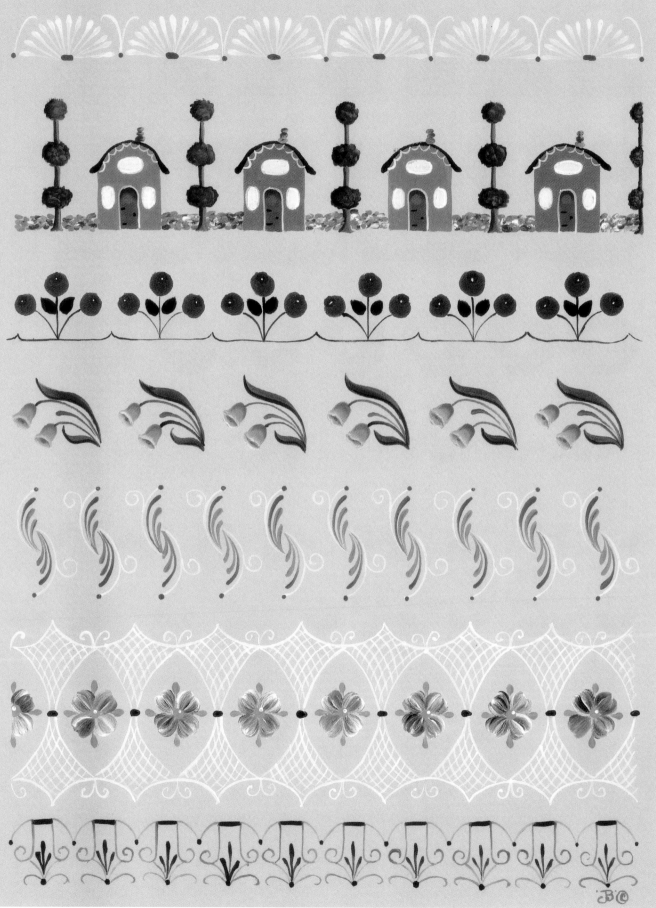

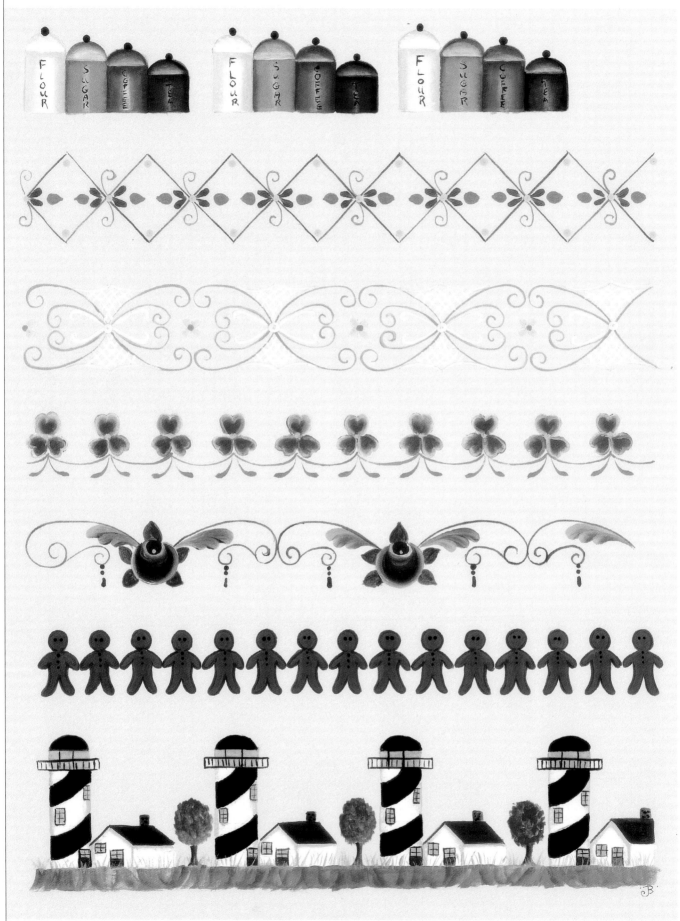

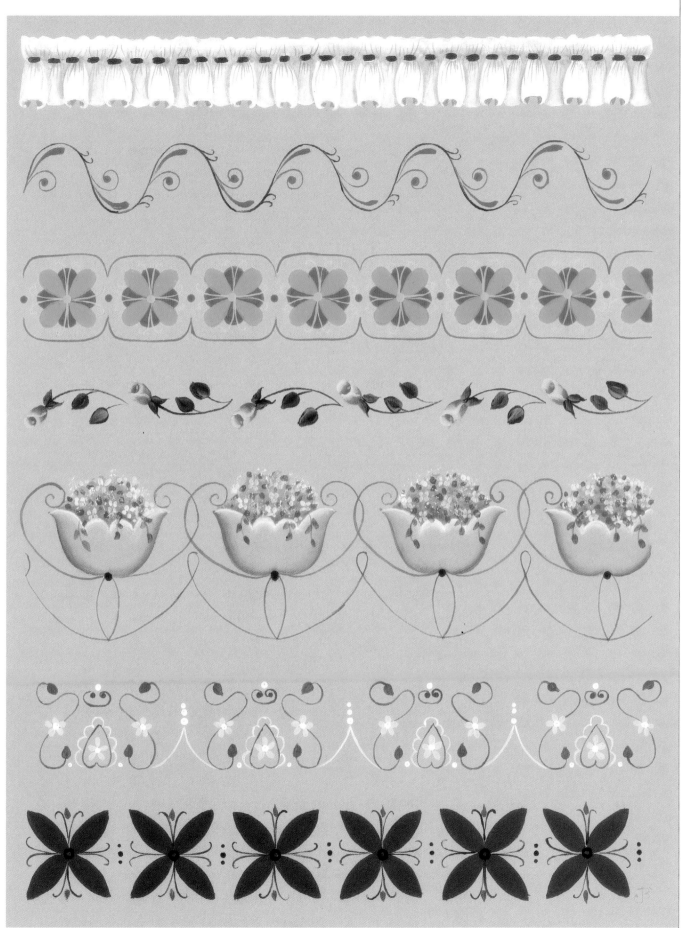

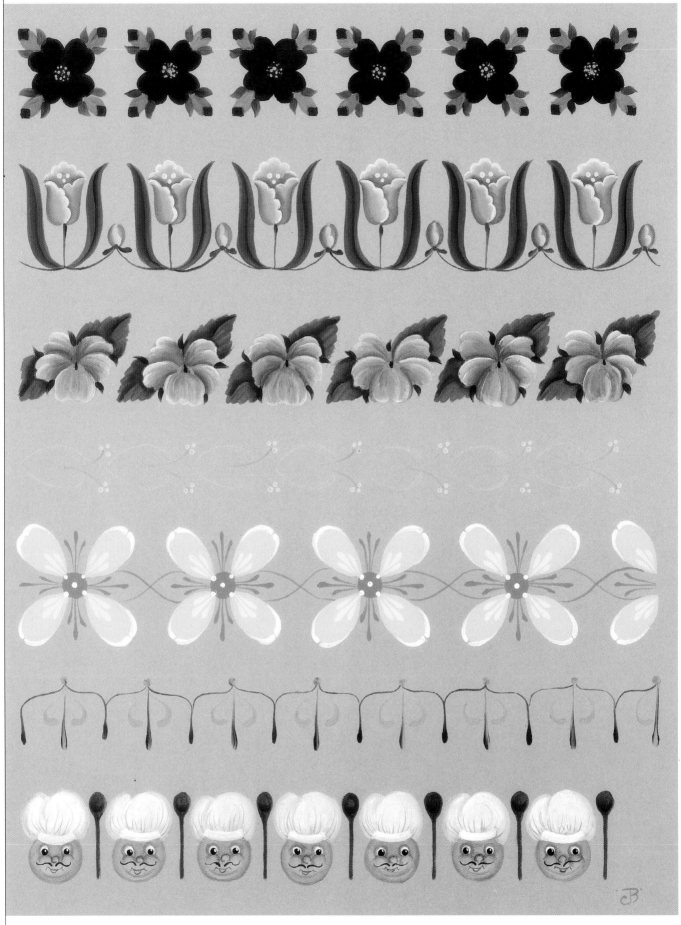

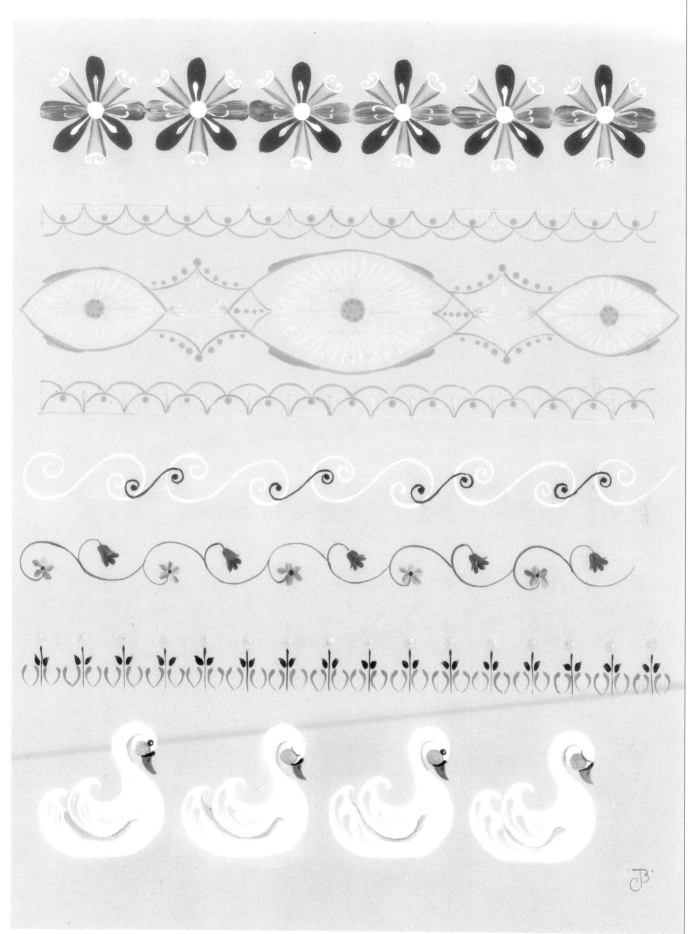

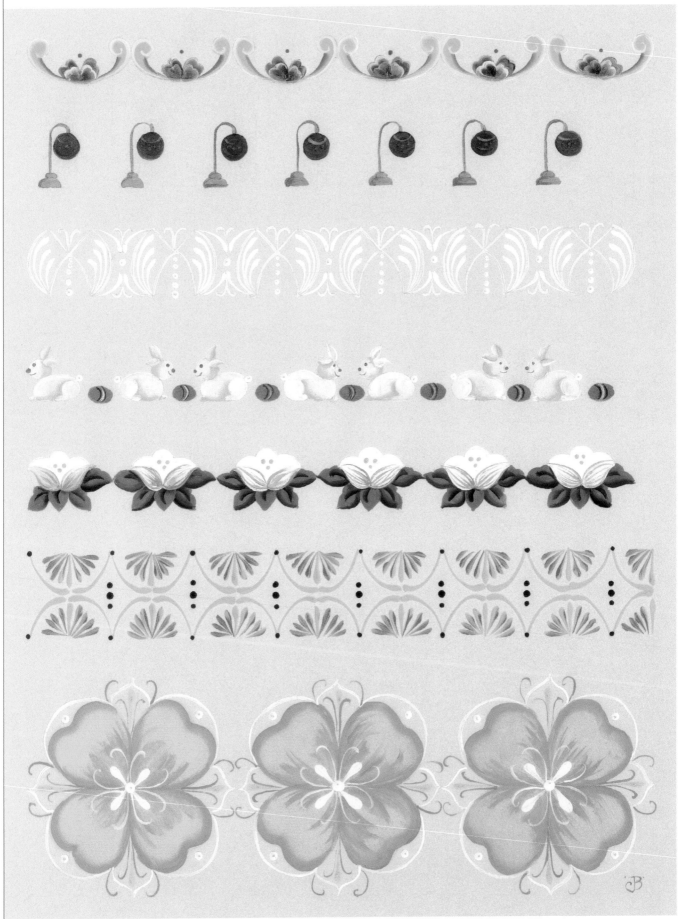

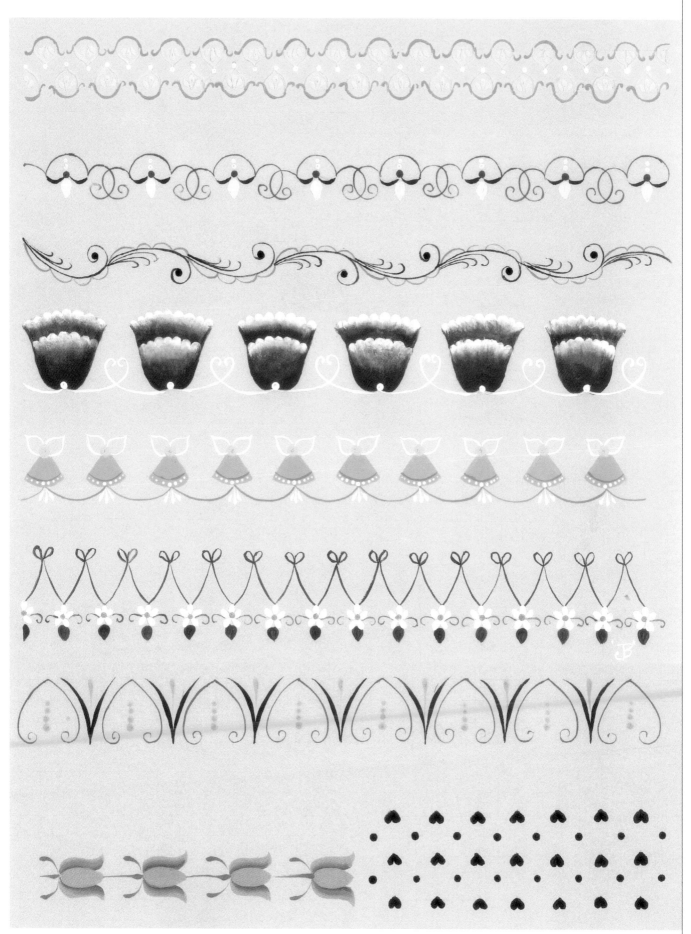

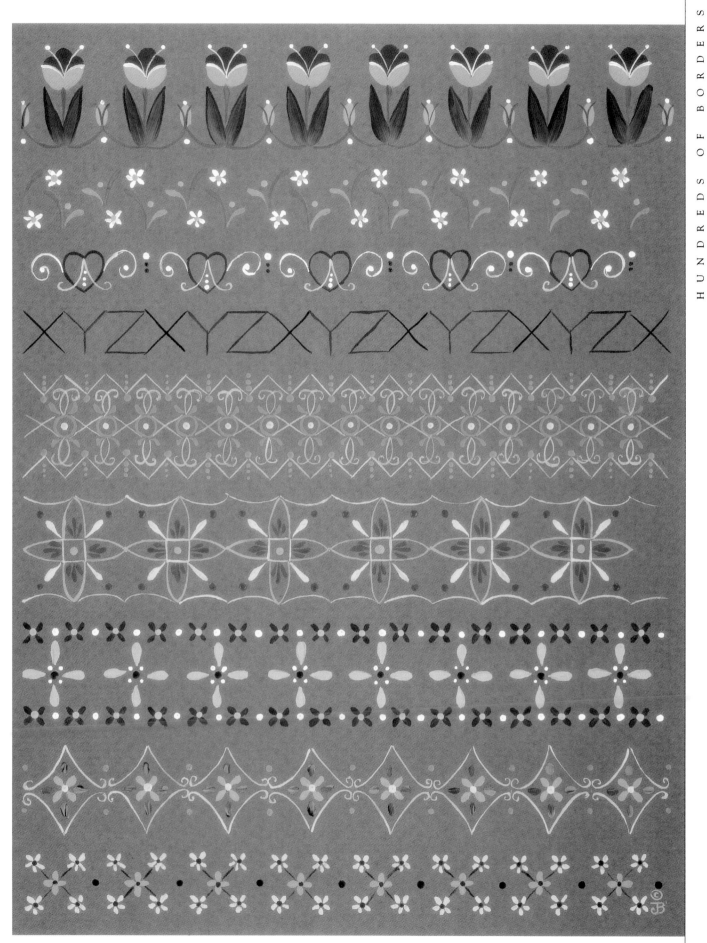

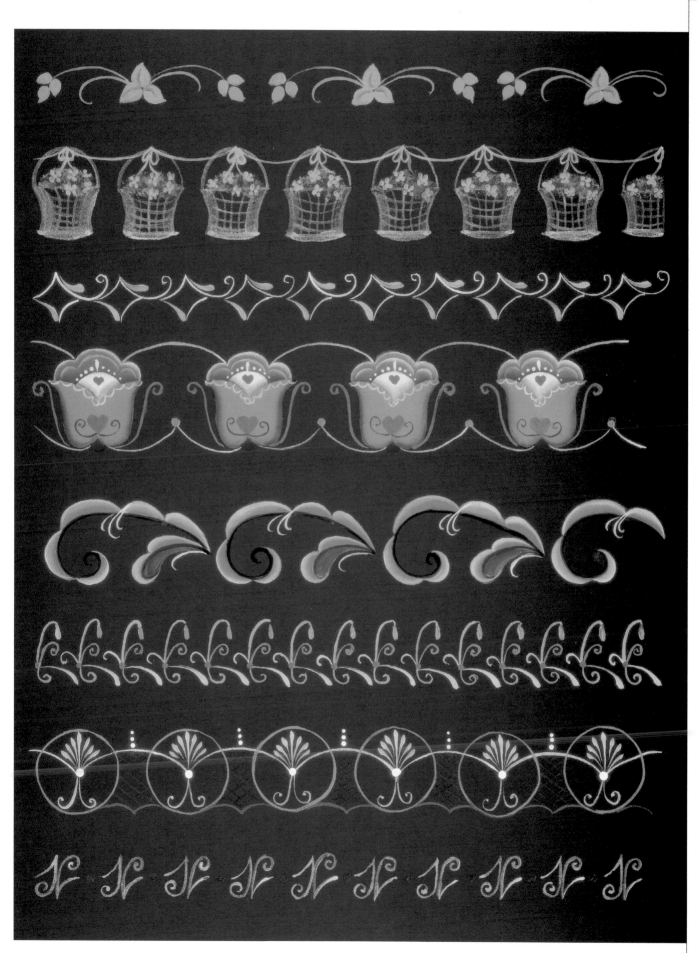

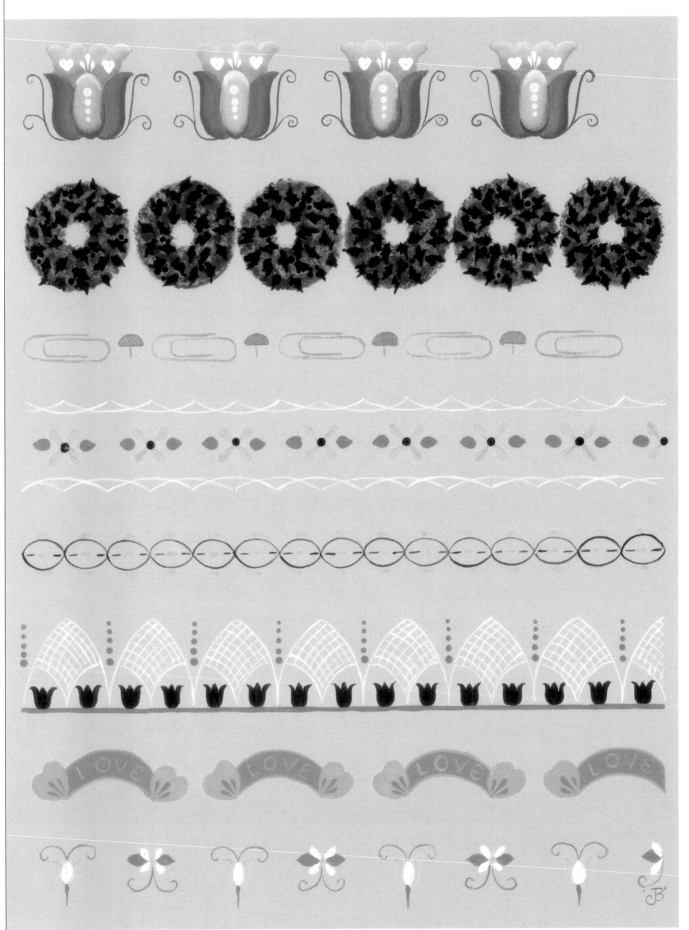

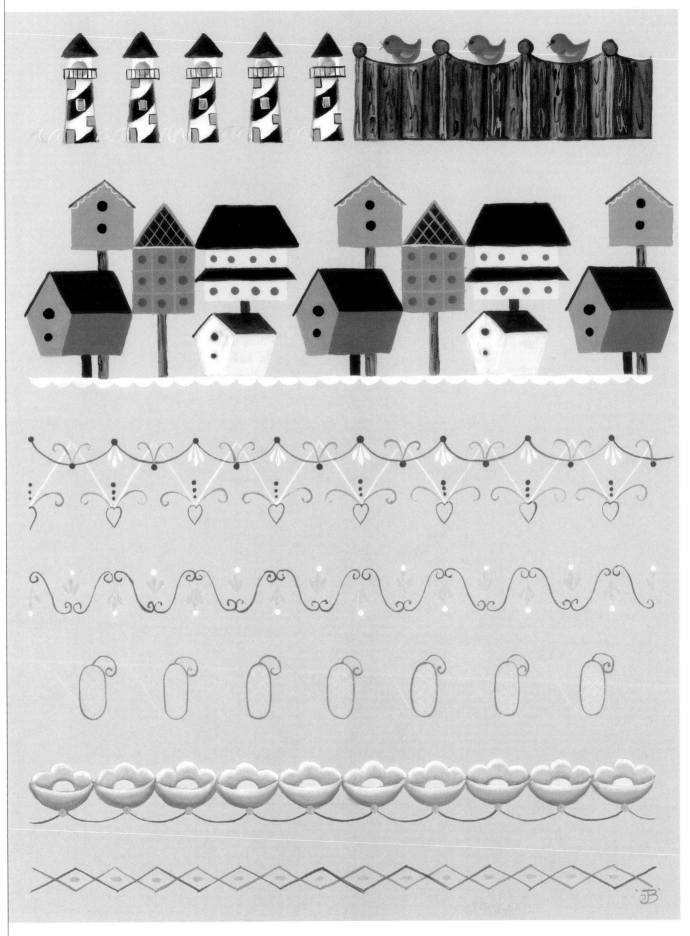

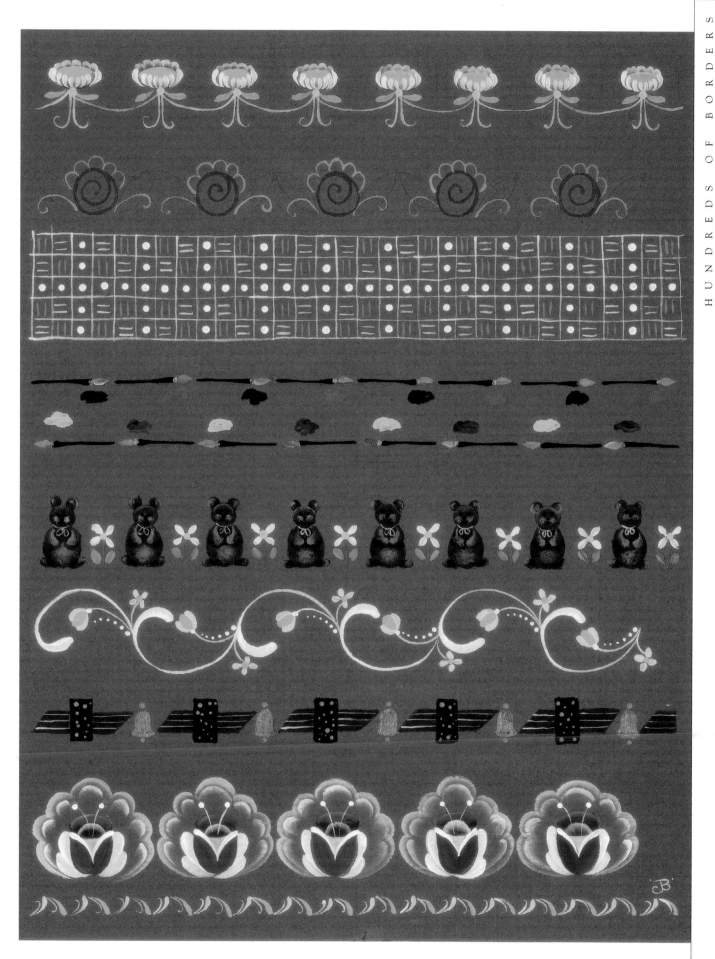

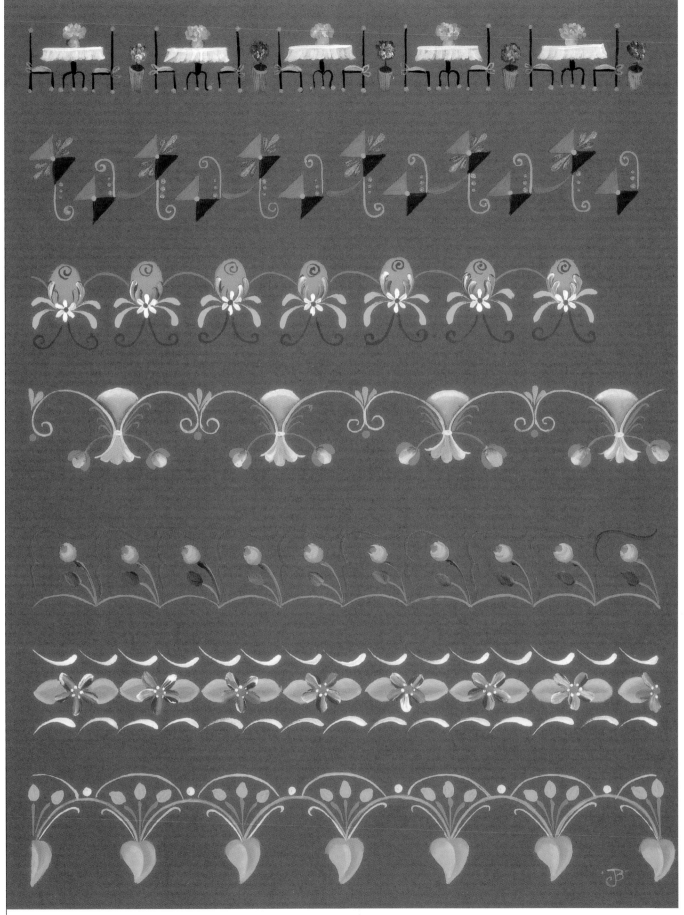

Patterns

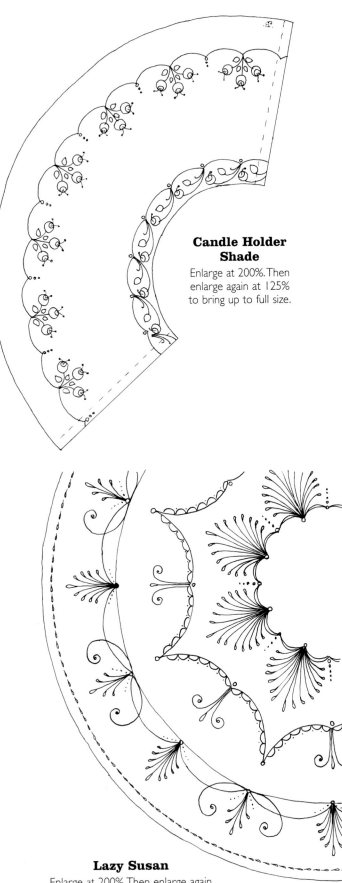

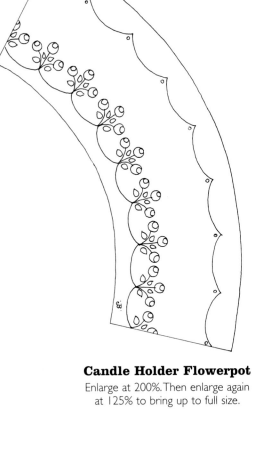

Candle Holder Shade

Enlarge at 200%. Then enlarge again at 125% to bring up to full size.

Candle Holder Flowerpot

Enlarge at 200%. Then enlarge again at 125% to bring up to full size.

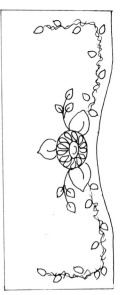

Lazy Susan

Enlarge at 200%. Then enlarge again at 125% to bring up to full size.

Letter Rack Front

Enlarge at 200%. Then enlarge again at 125% to bring up to full size.

134

Clock Frame

Enlarge at 200%.
Then enlarge again
at 125% to bring up
to full size.

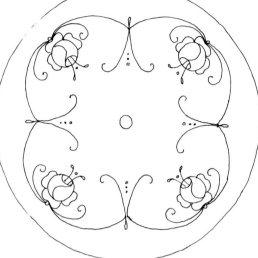

Clock Center

Enlarge at 200%. Then enlarge again at
125% to bring up to full size.

Letter Rack Side

Enlarge at 200%. Then enlarge again
at 125% to bring up to full size.

Place Mat

Enlarge at 200%. Then enlarge again
at 125% to bring up to full size.

Pie Basket Lid Border

Enlarge at 200%. Then enlarge again
at 111% to bring up to full size.

Pie Basket Lid Center

Enlarge at 200%. Then enlarge again at
111% to bring up to full size.

Pie Basket Inner Tray

Enlarge at 200%. Then enlarge again at 111% to bring up to full size.

Scrapbook Page

Enlarge at 200% percent to bring up to full size.

Note Cards

Enlarge at 200%. Then enlarge again at 111% to bring up to full size.

Pillowcase

Enlarge at 154% percent to bring up to full size.

Patterns

Wall Border

Enlarge at 167% percent to bring up to full size.

Trunk Side

Enlarge at 182% percent to bring up to full size.

Trunk Front

Enlarge at 182% percent to bring up to full size.

Trunk Lid

Enlarge at 154% percent to bring up to full size.

(Hinge side of trunk lid)

Resources

Brushes

Loew-Cornell, Inc.
563 Chestnut Avenue.,
Teaneck, NJ 07666-2491
201.836.7070
www.loew-cornell.com

Paints, Mediums and General Supplies

Delta Technical Coatings, Inc.
2550 Pellissier Place
Whittier, CA 90601
800.423.4135
www.deltacrafts.com

Surfaces

**Kunin Felt,
Foss Manufacturing Company Inc.**
380 Lafayette Road
P.O. Box 5000
Hampton, NH 03843-5000
603.929.6100
www.kuninfelt.com
(for Kreative Kanvas to make place mats)

Stan Brown Arts & Crafts
13435 NE Whitaker Way
Portland, OR 97230
800.547.5531
www.stanbrownartsandcrafts.com
(for clock, picnic basket and trunk)

Wildwood Park Associates
4232 Wildwood Drive
Medford, OR 97501
541.535.8301
(for lazy Susan)

**Eisenhart Wallcovering Co.
Technical Services**
www.eisenhartwallcoverings.com
(for Wall-Liner for Borders-use store locator on website)

The Sherwin-Williams Co.
www.sherwin-williams.com
(for Wall-Liner for Borders-use store locator on website)

Miscellaneous

Artograph, Inc.
2838 Vicksburg Lane North
Plymouth, MN 55447
888.975.9555
www.artograph.com
(for Globox lightbox)

American Traditional Designs
442 First NH Tpke.
Northwood, NH 03261
1.800.448.6656
consumers@americantraditional.com
(for "Hearts" brass embossing stencil)

Canadian Retailers

Crafts Canada
2745 29th Street NE
Calgary, AL, T1Y 7B5
403.219.0333

Folk Art Enterprises
P.O. Box 1088
Ridgetown, ON, N0P 2C0
800.264.9434

**MacPherson
Art & Crafts**
91 Queen Street East
P.O. Box 1810
St. Mary's, ON, N4X 1C2
800.238.6663
www.macphersoncrafts.com

**Maureen McNaughton
Enterprises Inc.**
Rural Route #2
Belwood, ON, N0B 1J0
519.843.5648
www.maureenmcnaughton.com

**Mercury Arts &
Crafts Supershop**
332 Wellington Road
London, ON, N6C 4P6
519.434.1636

**Town & Country
Folk Art Supplies**
93 Green Lane
Thornhill, ON, L3T 6K6
905.882.0199
www.artexpress.co.uk

UK Retailers

Art Express
Design House
Sizers Court
Yeadon LS19 6DP
0113 250 0077
www.artexpress.co.uk

Atlantis Art Materials
7-9 Plumber's Row
London E1 IEQ
020 7377 8855

Crafts World (head office)
No. 8 North Street, Guildford
Surrey GU1 4AF
Tel: 07000 757070

Green & Stone of Chelsea
259 King's Road
London SW3 5EL
020 7352 0837
www.greenandstone.com

HobbyCrafts Group Limited
7 Enterprise Way
Aviation Park
Bournemouth International Airport
Christchurch
Dorset BH23 6GH
0800 027 2387
www.hobbycraft.co.uk

HomeCrafts Direct
P.O. Box 38
Leicester LE1 9BU
0116 269 7723
www.homecrafts.co.uk

Index

The best in decorative painting instruction and inspiration is from North Light Books

The Complete Book of Decorative Painting

This book is the must-have one-stop reference for decorative painters, crafters, home decorators and do-it-yourselfers. It's packed with solutions to every painting challenge, including surface preparation, lettering, borders, faux finishes, strokework techniques and more! You'll also find five fun-to-paint projects designed to instruct, challenge and entertain you—no matter what your skill level. ISBN 1-58180-062-2, paperback, 256 pages, #31803-K

Handlettering for Decorative Artists

Overcome the challenge of handlettering with expert advice from Jackie O'Keefe. Featuring over 50 font alphabets to copy or trace, this book offers complete instructions for embellishing, sizing, transferring and painting. You'll find nineteen stroke-by-stroke examples that can be adapted for any decorative painting project. ISBN 0-89134-825-5, paperback, 128 pages, #31202-K

Fantastic Floorcloths You Can Paint in a Day

Want to refresh your home décor without the time and expense of extensive redecorating? Then painting canvas floorcloths is for you! Choose from 23 projects simple enough to create in a few hours. Designs range from florals to graphic patterns to holiday motifs, including some especially appropriate for kids' rooms. 12 accessory ideas inspire you to create a coordinated look. *Fantastic Floorcloths You Can Paint in a Day* makes adding creative touches to the home as easy as picking up a paintbrush. ISBN 1-58180-603-5, paperback, 128 page, #33161

Decorative Painting on Glass, Tiles and China

Carol Mays makes it easy to master the art of painting on glass, tile and china. You'll find surface, enamel and brush suggestions for getting started, information for oven-baking your art at home, and guidelines for cleaning and caring for your finished projects. You'll love her 15 fresh project designs, including floral, fruit, holiday and special occasion themes. Explore these exciting new painting surfaces and let your creative imagination shine! ISBN 1-58180-156-4, paperback, 128 pages, #31905

These books and other fine North Light titles are available at your local arts & craft retailer, bookstore, online supplier or by calling **1-800-448-0915** in North America or 0870 2200220 in the United Kingdom.